A Cloud of Witnesses

by Dan Schellenberg

All rights reserved, including the right of
reproduction in whole or in part in any form.

Copyright © 2012 by Dan Schellenberg

Published by Calvary Church
Landis Valley Road, Lancaster, PA 17601

Manufactured in the United States of America
ISBN 978-1-880976-20-3

Cover photo: John took this picture of Alice on their honeymoon while they were hiking high in the hills that let them look out for miles over the shimmering Athi Plains to the dark, forest – crested Machakos and Mua Hills ranges and on to Nairobi in the distant haze.

Contents

Preface 4

Chapter 1: My Conversion and Call To Missions 7

Chapter 2: An Incident in the South Atlantic 15

Chapter 3: In The Presence of My Enemies 24

Chapter 4: Africa At Last 34

Chapter 5: The Home of the Buffalo 43

Chapter 6: Marriage, Mambas and Malaria 55

Chapter 7: Paradise Lost and Regained 69

Chapter 8: Double-Edged Darkness 79

Chapter 9: A Royal Tea Party 91

Chapter 10: Farewell to Africa 99

Chapter 11: The Next-To-Last Chapter 107

Preface

The now famous author, Karen Blixen, a subject of the little kingdom of Denmark, writes in her diary, *Out of Africa*, that what drove her ambition and desire for adventure was the need that every human has to be observed in some detail. And, having been observed, perhaps loved to some degree. Which is to say that what she wanted more than fame or wealth was a "witness" to her life. She didn't need an entire audience, just one other person to "see" her, to "know" her, and to validate her.

Karen Blixen turned to Bror first, who only cared for her money. Then she turned to Denys Finch-Hatton, who treasured her mind but refused to marry her, although he proclaimed his love for her on the very morning he flew to have an affair with Beryl Markham (who wrote her remarkable story, *West with the Night*) when his plane crashed and he died at Tsavo. The power and meaning of Karen Blixen's life in some ways did not emerge until her book was made into a popular movie by the same name. Through that film, the whole world could "see" both her tragic heroism and the stunning landscape of her beloved, adopted country, Kenya.

There are numerous, and I dare say, far more heroic women's lives that remain uncelebrated who also chose the theater of Kenya for a backdrop to their drama. My mother was one of those women who held strong convictions about what sent her to Africa and service as a nurse in remote and often harsh locations. Having arrived in the country during the Second World War by nothing short of the miraculous, she fell in love with it and made it her heart's home. Kenya's incredible landscape and its endless herds of wildlife notwithstanding, Alice Schellenberg was on a mission.

Her mission, she would tell you, for nearly forty years, was to bring Christianity through medical care to native Africans. The more remote a station to which she was posted, the more satisfying it was to overcome the not inconsiderable administrative and social obstacles that seemed to block her work and on occasion nearly cost my mother her life and the lives of her four children.

My mother arrived in Kenya's raw, colonial culture just as America entered World War II, which at the time deprived her of any luxuries of food or "things" with which to entertain, which was a married woman's principle duty. And marry she did, promptly. Her plucky childhood on a Pennsylvania farm then served her well as she became famous for her food and for the cooks she trained, who never failed to end up as chefs in Nairobi's finest tourist hotels.

The list of her work and duties as a missionary, beyond that of being a wife and mother, is infinite. She literally wore herself out on numerous occasions trying to administer native schools, run rural clinics, teach women's religious classes and proper English etiquette, and somehow raise four children with the constant worry of snakes and disease. But, when it came to tea time, the trolley was always properly set. Perfect strawberry tarts and dainty sandwiches were served. Alice was no longer tired and frazzled, but a thoroughly composed hostess proudly welcoming her guests – pinky raised and everything quite proper!

Behind all of this "civility," however, lies a history of considerable suffering both physically and, in some ways, even more so emotionally. No summary sentence can fully capture this dark theme in the drama of her life. Her pain and disappointment were indescribable and apparently, almost uninterrupted for most of her early life in Africa. What she endured you have to read to believe. Why she stayed you must conclude for yourself. She would tell you that she went through it all for the glory of God, who loved her and called her personally to this place and ministry.

It has been my privilege in the ninety-eighth year of my mother's amazing life to become re-acquainted with her as an adult, to attend to her worthy story (both her words and her heart song), and to try to capture them in the brief vignettes and feeble lines that follow. While my parents were still serving in Kenya, my wife and I went there as missionaries ourselves and served in the same tribe, the aKamba, as they did. I have from that time an intimate acquaintance with many of her experiences and the language, geography and culture of Kenya. Two of my own children were born there.

In weaving her story to fit these pages, I have taken the liberty to abbreviate her history, although the key events follow chronologically. I have not in any way embellished the central experiences or her words that describe them. I have been surprised by the honesty and candor of her story. Her confidential sharing has been almost a confession, and I have written the details with what I trust is appropriate discretion.

I am grateful to my brother Steve for archiving the most treasured photos of our parent's earliest days in Kenya. My older sister, Joanne, has been invaluable in reading and refining this book, as she has clearer recollections of early childhood than I. She and my younger sister, Lois, have been devoted daughters, and both have spent many days and dollars caring for our mother for over twenty years during her retirement in Lancaster, Pennsylvania.

It is my hope in writing this book that I shall have been neither the first nor the last "witness" to Alice Schellenberg's fascinating life and personality. I pray that as the book is read more widely, a "cloud of witnesses" will bring her an added measure of peace and joy in the years ahead of her.

Dan Schellenberg
Kennard, Texas
December, 2011

CHAPTER 1
My Conversion and Call To Missions

I was only four years old when my father bought a farm just outside the community of Elizabethtown in the rolling hills of eastern Pennsylvania. There were eight children at that time, but there would soon be nine. It occurred to my father that a seventy-acre farm would be a far better place to raise his large family than a crowded house in town. The farm was within walking distance of both primary and secondary schools in Elizabethtown – although the walk in winter was often unpleasant, especially for us girls.

My father, Simon B. Landis, was the schoolteacher in the nearby town of Rheems. It was a two-room schoolhouse and my father taught the intermediate grades. He taught everything from math to history and biology. He was good at it and his talent for teaching was highly regarded in the community. But, it did not pay enough to support his family back then. So, during holidays, he turned his hand to construction and became a carpenter and a skilled cement finisher.

My older brothers helped with the farm chores, but my father basically rented the land to a sharecropper and kept some of the food to eat and some to sell. Pigs, chickens and a milk cow augmented our diet. My mother

Alice's father, Simon B. Landis and her mother, Alice Ebersole Landis, Elizabethtown, circa 1936.

canned everything – including the meat that the boys and Dad dressed every fall. My fondest memory of the place was drinking the pure, cold water that we pumped from the well. The farm was called Mt. Tunnel Farm because of a tunnel into the hillside for the train that rattled past our place many times every day.

My early life on the rural family homestead was in many ways idyllic, even though much of the time the country was caught in the grip of what we now call the Great Depression. We were made of stout Protestant stock. We worked hard and ate good food and left the rest to God – and the menfolk, who never ceased to quarrel over who was to blame for the economy and how to "fix the country."

My father was often asked to teach and preach in Mennonite churches, but after his trip to Europe, he came back with a far broader understanding of civil and religious liberty. He drove a car and did not force his girls or his wife to wear "plain" clothes or the standard-issue bonnets – required headcovering to show humility and submission to men – unless they were in church. He was famous for his slide shows of his trip to the historical sites of Europe.

It was just a matter of time before Simon Landis became too "modern" for the Mennonite church leadership. He was called up before a somber group of elders and given a chance to recant his modern practices – especially what they called showing "movies." He explained that they were slides. They "unchurched" him anyway. After that, my father simply spent his time on Sundays as an itinerant preacher, growing in popularity and getting paid for it, too.

As the second-to-last child – and a girl at that – I applied myself diligently to please my parents and achieved high marks in school. Miss Garber, my teacher for the first eight grades in a one-room schoolhouse, made learning a pleasure. I graduated from high school in the top of my class and then found I really liked nursing. In three years of training I excelled, which made it easy to find employment as a private-duty nurse in Lancaster, where I had completed my nursing training at St. Joseph Hospital from 1932 to 1935.

The family soon scattered, and I went home to Elizabethtown often to help my mother after my older sister, Mary, died in 1939. At my mother's feet, I learned to sew, embroider, cook and can, and also how to entertain elegantly on a shoestring. Little did I know how important this training would prove to be.

I was busy, to be certain. I had money. My pay for a twelve-hour day was $4, but I could buy 5 gallons of gas for a dollar back then. I did begin to date some interesting young men on occasion, but my life felt empty and without a real purpose. I harbored a secret fear of going to hell, which I had developed after reading a pamphlet in early elementary school. I did not want to die and go to hell, but I was not sure how to get to heaven. I went to church regularly – partially because of fear and partially out of habit. I thought I was good enough to be a Christian – certainly as good as the next person in the pew. My life was pretty routine at that time. And then, I moved further away from home to Norristown, to take a better-paying job at Montgomery Hospital.

Suddenly, I was really alone. In July of 1937, I began to date a young man I had met at a local evangelical church. He invited me to go to a special week of spiritual encouragement that included discussions about missions and spiritual discipline. I liked him and vaguely thought that what he suggested might be what I needed in order to have a more fulfilling personal life. We drove to a place in New Jersey called Keswick – an evangelical retreat center, it turned out. To this day, it remains a hallowed place on my spiritual pilgrimage.

I had no choice but to stay at Keswick, since my boyfriend dropped me off and had to return to work rather unexpectedly. This was fortuitous because I then had absolutely no distraction and soon came to grips with the understanding that I was not, in fact, a born-again believer. Every word of every message seemed directed at me. I had never heard such clarity of teaching in my life, and I was compelled to walk forward on the very first night to confess my sins and to receive Christ as my personal Savior.

As the preacher put it, my faith had moved from my head down to my heart that night. I felt light as a feather. My heart sang. I was free indeed, for the Truth had set me free! I was now saved and certain that my eternal destiny was in heaven. The gentle lady who counseled me and led me to faith in Christ filled out a small card to remind me of what I had done that night in July 1937. I kept it with me until it went down in the Atlantic with the *Zamzam* on my ill-fated first voyage to Africa.

After one morning session at Keswick that focused on missions, a woman spoke about a friend of hers in Africa, a nurse, who was forced to return to America because of poor health. Who would fill her place, the lady asked? The answer welled up in my heart. I would! It was as clear a call and response as I have ever had from my heart to the Spirit of God. I dedicated my life to serving Christ as a missionary in Africa that very moment. In offering medical service and the Gospel to the natives in darkest Africa, I had found a purpose for my life as a new believer.

I went back to Norristown transformed and within a week, resigned my job and went home – alone. It dawned on me that I was largely ignorant of Scripture. My Dad knew a great deal of God's Word, but it had not entered my heart by osmosis. I needed to study the Word of God myself. But where?

My older sister, Ruth, had gone to Moody Bible Institute in Chicago to prepare for a missionary career in India. Since that was the only conservative, evangelical Bible school I knew of, I applied for admission. It so happened that the dean of women at Moody had been a college friend of my father's at Millersville Teacher Training College in Pennsylvania. I think now that I was admitted so quickly in the fall of 1937 mostly on the merits of their friendship and her high regard for my father.

In any case, Moody allowed me to begin Bible training that year and I was able to find a nursing position in their clinic, which paid for my room and board. Moody never charged anyone tuition, trusting God to provide support for building upkeep as well as staff salaries. Two years flew by, and I was growing in my faith and enjoying my work and social life. I got to sing in various choruses and dated a few men who were bound for the mission field, as was I. A good number of students at Moody had been accepted by the Africa Inland Mission (AIM) to serve in Africa. I had applied to go to East Africa as a nurse with that mission, too. I felt very secure and supported in my desire to go to the mission field at Moody.

In the course of fulfilling their requirements for acceptance, I had to have a physical. While I felt strong and healthy, an x-ray exposed a lesion on one of my lungs. AIM required further tests. I was dismayed at first, but then one morning, I was having my devotions after the bad news, reading in the Gospel of Luke, chapter 12. There, before me, appeared verse 13, which said: "And Jesus said unto her, 'Woman, thou art loosed from thy infirmity.'"

Those words were spoken directly to me that morning, and I knew that I was healed. In my excitement, I ran down to see the AIM coordinator to tell him the good news. He sent a wire to AIM headquarters in New York, and they requested that I wait three months and then have another x-ray to prove this miracle. It was a surprise to the doctors and the mission directors that, indeed, my lesion was almost gone. It was not a surprise to me!

That little miracle was, however, not enough for AIM to accept me as a missionary nurse to Africa. They insisted that I also take a course in linguistics deep in the back woods of Arkansas, which they expected would test me physically and emotionally. I gladly took the bus to the Summer Institute of Linguistics (SIL) in Siloam Springs, Arkansas that summer. The place was a boot camp for missionaries, and the conditions were primitive even for that time of a depressed economy. To my surprise, I relished the camping style and hard work. The language study would turn out to be immensely helpful when I did finally get to Africa. My stay at SIL was a highlight of my preparation for mission service. Not only did I survive it, I truly thrived in that place. I was healthier and happier for that summer experience than I had ever been.

AIM finally accepted me for service in late 1940, and I set about packing the things friends and church folk supplied me that I thought I would need in primitive Africa. A friend who had come back from long-term work on that continent advised me well. She insisted that I take nice dishes and furnishings because I would be entertaining. If I happened to be stationed by myself, nice things would be cheerful when all around was drab. Her advice was surely prophetic, and I have given it to many other young couples myself over the years.

At last I was packed and headed to AIM headquarters in New York

City, accompanied by my parents and the pastor of the newly formed Calvary Independent Church on Duke Street in downtown Lancaster, Pennsylvania. Frank C. Torrey and the elders of this new church had graciously agreed to undertake my full support each month as well as to pay for my passage to the field.

The way it worked then, and still works, is that missionaries enter into a covenant with a local church, or a number of churches, for a certain amount of monthly support. AIM takes out a percentage for their overhead, pays Social Security taxes for retirement and holds other funds if they are requested – for example, transportation or travel funds.

I went up to my room at the AIM headquarters in New York on the farewell evening just before the service and put on a pink chiffon blouse, a dark skirt, my overcoat and finally, a new fedora hat with a feather in it. I wanted to look as good as I felt. Then, I remembered my older brother's advice to us girls. He said, "Be immaculate, then forget it!" This I did that evening.

It was a moving service, and the small crowd of well-wishers milling about in the warm light afterward seemed disinclined to leave. Suddenly, a group gathered around the piano and began to sing. I joined them, as did a young Canadian with a soft, tenor voice. He seemed shy, but he did agree to sing a duet with me when we were recognized by the group as having complementary voices. He was a lead tenor and I sang the harmonizing alto. The song we sang together that night would become the "theme song" of our life together: "I am resting, sweetly resting in the shelter of His love…."

The little flame that was lit in our hearts that night would not have much fuel beyond delayed letters to keep it bright for a few years. The next morning, I learned that one of my visas had not come in time for me to board the ship that was leaving that day. I stood on the dock with my family and, with a certain amount of shock and dismay, waved good bye to my new friends and one special man who stood on the deck, waving until the ocean liner passed the Statue of Liberty and became a smudge of smoke on the horizon.

I have to confess that I was confused and probably a bit upset with God for allowing this to happen after all the encouragement and guidance I had received. Was I misreading God's signals? The first morning after I returned to Mt. Tunnel farm to stay with my parents for a while and get my bearings, I turned to the Scripture to find an answer. Without really thinking, I opened my Bible up to John 13:7. There, I read the startling words: "What I do thou knowest not now, but thou shalt know hereafter." That admonition was all I needed to relax and trust God to work out my passage to Africa and show me what I must do in the meantime.

In about a month, just around the time I would have been arriving in Kenya, my mother came into the parlor after lunch, complaining of nausea and a severe headache. She lay down on the couch and suddenly began to spit up blood, convulsing for some time. I rushed to get a basin and then called the doctor. My dad drove us to the hospital, where mother underwent surgery for ruptured ulcers. I cared for my mother for a few weeks after her surgery, but she developed peritonitis and died. This was in early 1940's and antibiotics were not yet being used.

The Lord's timing finally did make sense! I was so grateful for the added days I got to spend with my mother and to be with her at the end of her life. She and Dad are both buried in the Schaeffer Cemetery in Elizabethtown, right next to my husband, John.

The Simon Landis family at their Mt. Tunnel farm, circa 1929. (l to r front) Elsie, Edith, Mother, Dad, Mary. (l to r back) Alice, Walter, John, Amos, Ruth, Albert.

After mother's death, my dad sold the farm and home and moved in with his son, Amos, at the Masonic Homes in Elizabethtown where my brother ran the orchards and cider mill. When I asked Dad why, he simply replied that he did not want to obligate me to stay and care for him. It was important to him that I be able to obey God's calling for my life. He would not stand in my way if I still wanted to go. I did still want to go.

I was thrilled to be going to the mission field. And, I was ready – regardless of the threat to maritime shipping in the south Atlantic created by what can only be described as German pirates having their way on the high seas.

CHAPTER 2

An Incident in the South Atlantic

My visas and my passport were at last in order, and the AIM office advised me that a neutral passenger liner was set to sail for Mombasa, Kenya, shortly. I packed my suitcases and a large trunk with all the essential things I felt I would need for a life in the African bush. We loaded up the family car and traveled from Elizabethtown to New York City one windy, cold March day in 1941.

After spending the night at the AIM headquarters on Pearl Street in Brooklyn, New York, we reloaded the family car and set out for the pier. A knot of what turned out to be Egyptian sailors helped me carry my things up the gang-plank and down to my stateroom. The ship – the *Zamzam* – was an old British WWI troop ship converted by the Egyptians into a passenger liner plying the coast of Africa. It was not a thing of beauty, hanging low in the oily water with no flags flying to betray its nationality.

The ship's steam horn on the sooty smokestack gave a blast, and we went on deck to wave good-by to what was now a crowd of family and well-wishers from the mission offices and the church in Lancaster.

The Egyptian liner Zamzam, *shown above at Jersey City, New Jersey, just before sailing on its fateful voyage.*

They broke into song as the crew untied the ropes and a tug pushed us from the quay. The warm, comforting melody of "Lead Kindly Light" wafted up to us on the chill wind, and I joined the other one hundred or so missionaries on the deck in singing along. It was hard for the excited group to hold back the tears as we passed the great Statue of Liberty in the harbor. A billow of smoke and a shudder from the engines got us moving into open water as we turned south to Baltimore to pick up one hundred tons of nitrate fertilizer – ostensibly to grow cotton in Egypt.

We heard rumors that evening that the holds up front were filled with brand new ambulances and other contraband. Young American ambulance crews composed of the sons of the wealthy and famous were headed for the war in North Africa in support of the British forces headquartered in Cairo. They made themselves quite visible and quickly showed their contempt for the missionaries on board. They called us "sky pilots." America was not yet engaged in the war directly, but our sympathies, quite obviously, lay with Great Britain. These privileged young men must have known what we did not – that our country was heading to war, and they would not have to be on any front in harm's way.

The next day, after loading the fertilizer, the *Zamzam* steamed on south into warmer weather and very calm seas to Trinidad. We got off there and enjoyed the fruit and good food as our ship took on water and supplies for the voyage across the Atlantic. The next day, to our consternation, we headed even further south to Recife, Brazil – called Pernambuco then. To this day, I cannot fathom what required us to visit this port. We did pick up two passengers – one a *Life* magazine photographer, David Scherman, and the other a journalist and editor of *Fortune* magazine, Charles Murphy. They pretty much kept to themselves or spent time with the other "non" missionaries. They were bound for North Africa as well to document the war for their American audience. Those two men were to play an important role in making life bearable after we all became prisoners of the Germans.

On the morning of April 8, 1941, the *Zamzam* slowly churned its way out of Recife port and began to steam due east toward South Africa, weeks away at the top speed of 13 knots. I and my cabin comrades went up on deck to witness the departure of our rather untidy ship from the last spit of land. It felt good to be finally sailing toward our destination, yet we could not shake the sense of concern heading out to rough seas in this rust bucket. And then, suddenly, as if God had anticipated that little shadow of worry that came over us, a brilliant, wide rainbow appeared over the harbor as if to remind us that no matter what happened, we were in God's faithful care.

For two full weeks, the gloomy crew of Egyptians and Somalis busied themselves with cleaning and painting the ship. We Protestant missionaries met to sing and hold our daily prayer meetings and the Catholics held their masses just as faithfully. The food wasn't great, but it offered a break from sitting on deck watching the ship's frothy wake or napping. The Atlantic Ocean seemed immense, dark and cold. These were shark-infested waters. For the first few weeks, however, the weather was delightful and the warm sunshine kept us in high spirits.

The first scare we had came on the night after we had been sailing for two weeks. We had been traveling under blackout conditions from Recife, but suddenly, just about tea-time one afternoon, the ship stopped and turned abruptly. We found out much later that another ship about

20 miles away had radioed an SOS signal for help since it was apparently being tailed by a German surface raider. Our captain, a rugged Scotsman, dared not send out a reply or he would give away his own position. We began to zigzag all over the ocean, steaming as slowly as we could by day so as not to send up a massive cloud of dark smoke and an invitation to follow us, also. At night, the tired old ship fairly groaned as the captain put on as many miles as the engines could manage.

Rumors were fairly flying one afternoon a few days later. Some thought we had been betrayed by the Egyptians. Others thought we were carrying contraband that the Germans would see as loyalty to the British. After supper that evening, most of the missionaries gathered for devotions on the deck. The air was calm, the moon bright, and there was a strange sense of peace and quietness. I made up my mind, however, not to be unprepared in case of an attack.

I went alone back to the cabin and sorted through my things. I wanted to take my Bible, for sure, and my important papers and some money. I laid out a wool suit with a jacket. The suit would dry quickly if I ended up in the water, and I could remove the jacket in the sun and put it back on in the cold night air. Finally, I decided to carry an um-

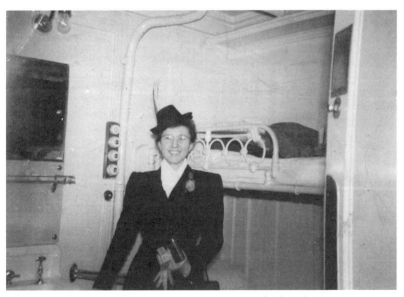

Alice next to her bunk in her Zamzam stateroom just after boarding.

brella, which would provide vital shade from the blistering sun and I could use it to catch rain if I turned it upside-down. I collected my little emergency kit and felt as prepared as I could be.

Just before dawn the next morning, I awoke to the sound of a loud whine that crescendoed into an earsplitting shriek and an explosion so loud and so close to our cabin that it almost knocked me off my feet. The No. 4 lifeboat just outside our cabin had saved my life before I could even get in it! It fell to the deck in splinters. I pulled on my "emergency" clothes and rushed to the port-hole to see what I could see. On the horizon, in the eerie dawn light, what I saw was a cloud of smoke punctuated by a tiny orange flame every few seconds, followed by a whine and a crash that made the entire vessel shudder. Nothing was so unnerving as that whine, for I knew that in the next few seconds, I could die.

The German raider was, I would learn later, ten miles away and steaming at us with its six-inch guns blazing. At six miles, the raider found its range and began to hit us regularly – eight times in all. We also learned later that the raider had fired fifty-five rounds in our direction. Were they bad shots or was there a divine hand interfering? The radio tower near the bridge was an early target to destroy any chance of sending an SOS and giving away the raider's position. With the *Zamzam* isolated and taking on water, our captain finally turned broadside to the raider and surrendered.

As I found my way to the open deck, I was shocked to see the devastation and chaos. The ship was already listing to port, where shells and four torpedoes had blasted gaping holes in the hull above and below the water line. The Egyptian crew had dutifully dropped several lifeboats, which they promptly filled themselves to get away from the sinking *Zamzam*. Life rafts were thrown overboard, and many people slid down ropes into the remaining lifeboats or swam to the gently bobbing rafts. The sea was calm and the sun bright. I felt a sense of peace even as I climbed into one of the last lifeboats to be let down. There was a family with small children and an elderly couple in the boat with us.

We hit the ocean and the boat immediately began taking on water. In the confusion of abandoning ship, someone had failed to put the plug in the bottom of the lifeboat. We could not bail fast enough to keep it afloat with everyone on board. There was nothing to stuff in

Passengers abandoning the listing Zamzam *after it was shelled by the German raider, the* Atlantis.

the hole. The young family and the old couple needed to stay and bail, so we few single women agreed to get into the water and swim to a raft we could see. We thought our getting out would lighten the boat and give the families a little more time. We did not know what the German raider would do with us at that time.

I slid into the water. I was surprised to find that it was not as cold as I had expected. I was a good swimmer, but it quickly became clear that I could not swim holding the box of important things as well as my Bible and my umbrella. In the next moment, I dropped everything, placed the loop of the umbrella handle over my wrist and began to swim to the nearest raft. Nothing mattered to me at that point except survival. All of it quickly became irrelevant and replaceable.

As I climbed onto the rough planks of the raft, I heard a sort-of loud sighing and sounds of surprise from those all around me. On the horizon, over the stricken ship, a brilliant rainbow appeared. God was still in charge and would keep His promise. And, He did! Not a single one of the nearly 200 persons on the *Zamzam* died during the shelling. Some were badly wounded and one eventually died, but no one would dispute that we had experienced a miracle. Isaiah 41:10 kept repeating in my mind as we floated in the early-morning sun that sparkled on the calm sea and I rested in the shade of my green umbrella: "Do not fear, for I will be with you. I will help you. Surely I will uphold you with my right hand."

We floated in those shark-infested waters and watched as the German crew finally sent out a flotilla of launches to rescue those who were swimming and those who were clinging to capsized lifeboats. The German raider had moved very close in among us and we could see its name, the *Tamesis* painted on its bow. It flew a Norwegian flag. Little did we know that this was the most famous and most feared surface raider in the German fleet. Looming above us was, the *Atlantis*!

Its crew could change the ship's identity in minutes, and even enter hostile ports for water and supplies. Great guns were camouflaged as cranes over the holds that further concealed heavy machine guns. Below, there were ports from which to launch torpedoes. It took the

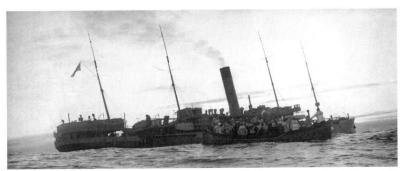

Ten minutes after shelling by the Nazi raider stopped, Scherman (in lifeboat #1) took this picture of the stricken Zamzam *with another lifeboat pulling toward open water.*

German crew nearly all morning to collect the passengers in the water and get everyone on deck. To get to the deck of the raider, we had to climb ropes.

Climbing up those rope ladders was dangerous and accomplished only because of heroic effort on the part of all survivors. Children and the wounded were hauled up in rope baskets, but most of us climbed a knotted rope ladder with no help. I clung for dear life to the rope and prayed my umbrella would not fall from my arm. It seemed like an hour, but I finally hoisted my body over the railing and caught my breath on the deck – umbrella in hand!

Realizing that they had shelled a neutral ship carrying many American passengers, the captain and crew took every measure to ensure we were treated well. They sent their launches for several hours to the *Zamzam* to collect our personal belongings. The deck of this hostile raider looked like an Egyptian *Souk* for a time as we combed through piles of clothing and belongings. Some found musical instruments and family photos; I found a packet of letters given to one of my cabin mates to be doled out to me as we progressed toward Africa – a steady supply of encouragement and spiritual support.

The women and children were herded into crew quarters and the library. Dry clothes and blankets were welcome. There was even lemonade ladled out to the children on deck. The German crew never once made any untoward move to harass us women or the children. They were stern but kind and remained aloof from us prisoners. The men were taken below into a hold, where it became clear that this effort at rescuing survivors was not the first for this ship. There were enough bunk beds and toilets for all of them.

It wasn't long before we were all marshalled on deck. The handsome captain of the *Atlantis* addressed us in perfect English from the bridge. He had sent out a crew to plant depth charges in the *Zamzam* and in a half-hour, they would explode and she would sink, he told us. We all stood there in silent disbelief. And then, just as he had said, at about 3 o'clock that afternoon, three huge plumes of water shot into the sky and the broken hull of the ill-fated *Zamzam* disappeared forever under the dark Atlantic Ocean.

A silent and somber group of missionaries gathered in the shadow of the smokestack to sing and pray. Then, we made our way to the rooms that would be our sleeping quarters to organize the mattresses and sort out the things we had collected from the *Zamzam*.

Supper was a surprise and a warm relief. The German crew served us hot soup with a piece of dark bread and a slice of sausage. We even had a cup of sweet tea to wash it all down. Eating that food serves as the single most memorable meal of my life. Whenever I recall it, the words from Psalm 23 become very real and personal: "Thou preparest a table before me in the presence of mine enemies." It seems that we humans only really understand the full power of Scripture through such extreme experience.

CHAPTER 3
In The Presence of My Enemies

Early the next day, after our shelling and rescue, we were somewhat alarmed to see a large ship steaming directly at us. But, the fact that the *Atlantis* took no evasive action helped us to calm down. The ship turned out to be a supply ship, the *Dresden*. We were all to be transferred to it and taken to some neutral port and sent back to America, the captain informed us. The English and Canadian missionaries, however, faced a different fate. They would be sent to prison camps, which turned out to be the now-infamous Dachau and Buchenwald.

The transfer of some 200 prisoners from the *Atlantis* to the *Dresden* was to be accomplished by having us all walk down a make shift gang-plank that stood in a pitching launch with two sailors balancing in it to steady us. Once in the small boat, we were obliged to clamber up another rickety catwalk to get to the deck of the *Dresden*. That no one was hurt or drowned in this ordeal was a miracle of no less proportion than the original rescue by the *Atlantis*. It took all day for both crews to move our belongings – such as they were – once all of us prisoners had managed the crossing.

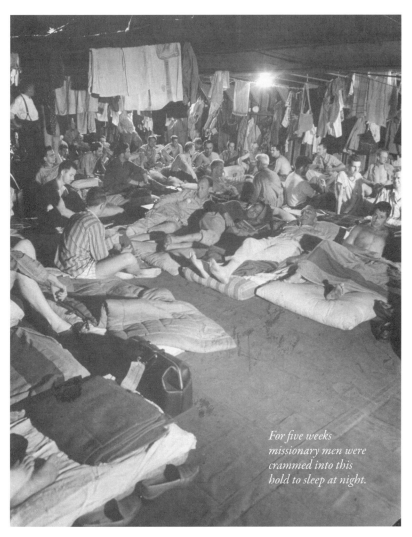

For five weeks missionary men were crammed into this hold to sleep at night.

To our dismay, the *Dresden* was not a ship capable of anything close to hospitality. We women did have more privacy in the crew quarters than the men, whom they stowed in the holds. Our plumbing worked, but the men had to build their own latrines on the aft deck, with only a privacy curtain of blankets. The first morning on our prison ship, the captain mustered all souls on deck and informed us that we were his prisoners and that he expected "no monkey business" or he would have us shot. His warning would have been comical except that he seemed entirely serious about curbing the "threat" from this unarmed collection of bedraggled missionaries intent solely on staying alive. We represented no challenge to this tough sailor or his crew, but the size of our group must have unnerved him.

The food on the prison ship was not just boring for its repetition, but close to inedible. In the morning, we were served a watery paste of cooked flour gruel from a huge cauldron. For lunch and dinner, they alternated between rice with soup and then in the evening, it was pasta again with watery soup. Whichever was served at noon, we got the other that night. We affectionately called the meals, "billboard paste and glop," both notable for their consistency and absence of any taste – or nutrition, for that matter. Not a sign of any meat or vegetable did we observe in the soup the entire five weeks on that prison ship. In a form of ironic reversal, the Germans insisted that the male prisoners serve us women our meals in the lounge and then clean up, too. This chivalry did not continue once our men were free from German authority!

After a few days of listless lying around, singing and chatting with each other, it became obvious that we were not going to be dropped off at some friendly port any time soon. We prisoners had a petition drawn up to present to our captor in which we pleaded with him to drop us quickly at a neutral port. He ignored it – probably because he had other orders. The days grew into weeks and boredom set in. The teachers among the prisoners finally got organized and began to hold "school" for the older children. Oddly enough, some musical instruments had been salvaged and a group of musicians entertained the ship as often we could coax them to play. But we needed something—a project—that would occupy the women for days.

Since David Scherman and Charles Murphy had become somewhat the favorites of the German captain, they were sent to discover what could be done to occupy the women. They turned up some sewing machines and a constant supply of food sacks that we quickly turned into large bags for carrying our belongings. A small industry fairly mushroomed around this enterprise, and many of us were proud to display our bags when we finally got back to America. It was the *Zamzam* look! Needless to say, it did not become a hit in New York fashion circles.

We zigzagged over the Atlantic for a month or more, blacked out at night and steaming hard to make up time lost in daylight. Then suddenly, one evening, the captain ordered us to sleep in our clothes and have our life jackets ready to put on quickly. We could only imagine that we were going to be shelled again. As I went to bed that first night under this new threat, I opened a letter in my rescued packet. In it, I found a poem that seemed exactly timed for this moment:

> *"No shell nor bomb can on me burst*
> *Except my God permit it first.*
> *Then let my heart be kept in peace,*
> *His watchful care will never cease,*
> *No bomb above, nor mine below,*
> *Need cause my heart one pang of woe:*
> *The Lord of Hosts encircles me,*
> *He is the Lord of earth and sea."*

The next afternoon, the captain ordered our guards to escort us into two holds—women and children in one and men in the other. Once all his prisoners were locked up, he posted an armed guard. We all feared that we were finally under attack and would die in those hot, steel cages. We waited for the tell-tale whine of some fateful shell. To our great relief, none came.

The next morning, a cheerful officer let us out, and we mustered on deck to hear the captain explain that we were going to run the British blockade and that he would not be responsible for our deaths if we were shelled by the British fleet – its boats were thick in these waters along the coast of Europe at that time. Off in the distance, we could see the dark shape of the Pyrenees mountains. "Unto the hills shall I lift up mine eyes, from whence cometh my help," went through all our minds.

Rumors were fairly flying the next day when we sighted a fingernail sliver of shoreline. Over the horizon, a third and final rainbow appeared as if to promise us one last time that God was watching over us still. All of us crowded on deck to watch as the bit of sand grew into an empty beach. A sudden lurch and shudder told us our ship had run aground. Shortly thereafter, we were told to climb down the familiar ropes into launches for a ride up a narrow channel to the ramshackle beach of St-Jean-de-Luz. Our new handbags served us well as we rowed ashore with all our earthly possessions in them, grateful to be on *terra firma* after such a very long time at sea.

We were to learn much later that the ease with which the *Dresden* ran the blockade with two minesweepers in tow was due to the fact that German U-boats had sunk the celebrated British battleship *Hood*, just the day before. Every British boat was out at sea hunting the German warships that had done this terrible deed. We had slipped into occupied France in the chaos. The minesweepers tried vainly to dislodge the grounded *Dresden* but to no avail. The angry captain then reversed engines full, swung his boat hard to port and dislodged himself from the shoal. Perhaps without the 190 prisoners, his ship was finally light enough to float—a gift of freedom he now shared with us – but one he truly did not deserve.

St-Jean-de-Luz was a small town that had the misfortune to straddle the Spanish-French border, but was considered by the Germans to be occupied France. As soon as we got out of the small boats, I and my two cabin friends climbed onto an open truck for a trip through the French countryside to the resort of Biarritz. What a surprise awaited us at the end of our dusty ride!

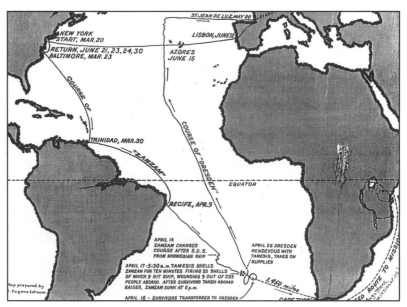

Eugene Johnson drew this map of the route taken by the Zamzam to its grave and then the course of the prisoners to Europe and their return to the United States.

Biarritz had been once the playground of the rich and famous in France before the war, and we were probably housed there to make the embarrassment of having sunk so many Americans on the high seas more palatable to the American government. Because of the war, however, the resort was full of German officers on R&R leave. America was still not at war at that time, yet we were considered prisoners, so we were accommodated in the lower-class wings and rooms of this resort. It was nice enough. My old cabin mates joined me in a cubby-hole of a room. But, the size of the room didn't matter. We were free to walk about the grounds after a few days of quarantine and took full advantage of the nearby beach—enjoying the fresh air and solid ground beneath us. The food we got was not *haute cuisine* by any stretch of the imagination, but after billboard paste and glop, we ate it gladly! I even put on a little weight – not unnoticed by my friends when I got back to New York.

The very next morning following our arrival at Biarritz, the American ambassador drove down from Bordeaux, France, to meet us. His cable back to New York that we were all alive and well was the first confirmed assurance my family had of my safety since they had heard the news of the sinking of the *Zamzam* five weeks earlier. My father got the

Passengers from the Zamzam were crammed into this truck for transport to a resort hotel at Biarritz.

cable and wanted to reply to me with brief encouragement. He typed in, Romans 8:28, which the postmaster promptly refused to send as he concluded it was some secret code. Little did he know what that code meant! "All things work together for good to those who love God and are called according to His purpose."

The ambassador began the long process of reissuing our passports. As we sat waiting our turn to talk to him, the Germans herded the Canadians and British among us into trucks for the long journey to internment deep in Germany. It mattered not to them that they were separating husband from wife and parents from their children. Kisses flew over the barbed wire fences and we watched until the dust obliterated the sad convoy, which we were certain was destined for death. The tears that flowed could have re-floated the *Dresden*.

Only after the war did we learn that not a single one of those passengers from the *Zamzam* died in German concentration camps. In fact, when I finally did get to Kenya, a letter surfaced from Clara Guilding (the wife of our future Machakos station chairman, John Guilding) written while both of them were in Dachau. In her letter, Clara asks the Red Cross to send her a Bible. This they did. American soldiers eventually set them free, and they both then made their way to Kenya and lived long and productive lives there.

The American Red Cross showed up at Biarritz that first week and gave us bags of free toiletries. It was nice to smell good and feel clean again. We had no money and no papers, so we were as good as imprisoned. We asked the Red Cross to lend us some money, which they finally agreed to do, but not until we had each signed a piece of paper promising to repay every cent we borrowed when we got back to the United States.

With time on our hands and money to burn, we single ladies ventured into the French town nearby. The people were wary but not unfriendly. We talked to them in English and they shrugged and answered in muttered French. I wanted to buy some clothes and a decent pair of shoes, but that was not to be. I did buy an authentic French beret, however, which I proudly wore the rest of the trip. In the end, I owed my government via the Red Cross "loan" a total of $316.21 for my adventure in Europe and my passage to back to New York.

At last, the day dawned when we were to leave Biarritz for a long and uncomfortable train ride to Spain and then on to Portugal, where we would take a ship from Lisbon to New York. Once into Spain, however, we single girls got bumped back into the third-class section of the train with peasant families and all their goats and vegetables. It was miserable and it was impossible to sleep with the noise and lurching while perched uncomfortably on a wooden bench.

At San Sebastian, Spain, the train suddenly stopped. We were all asked to disembark and to our amazement, there on the platform before us was spread a sumptuous feast. Our first instinct was to shove as much food into our pockets as we could and then we ate until we fairly burst. What good food it was! I can still taste that fresh bread! To this day, I have no idea what prompted such hospitality to strangers in the middle of nowhere during a war.

Back on the train, we went on to the quaint town of Sintra, a few miles from Lisbon. There, we *Zamzam* refugees were put up in four hotels until we could get all our travel documents in order. The American ambassador did his best to assure us that we would soon be home and safe, and that we would not be sunk on an American ship during the return journey to America. He was quite unaware of who we really trusted for our safety. To those who insisted on going on to take up their posts in Africa, he gently demurred. Not a chance for any more trouble on his watch!

As I reflected one warm evening during my devotions while in Sintra, the verses from Psalm 105:13-15 came to mind: "When they went from one nation to another, from one kingdom to another people; He suffered no man to do them wrong; yea, He reproved kings for their sakes; saying, Touch not mine anointed and do my prophets no harm." I took great comfort that God would go before me and prepare the way safely for the rest of my journey.

Finally, on June 10, 1941, we boarded a huge, Portuguese passenger liner (neutral, but not American) crowded with over 700 people bound for New York. Part of the reason we twenty-six single ladies from the *Zamzam* got passage on this ship was that there were over one hundred Jewish refugee children among the 734 passengers. The *Zamzam* missionaries were asked to befriend them and possibly teach them some English during the voyage. They were mostly middle-school-aged children, but they were bright and eager to learn. They demonstrated remarkable resilience given the terrible circumstance of knowing their parents were in concentration camps behind barbed wire – and now an ocean would separate them further.

The crammed liner, named the *Mouzinho*, sailed from Lisbon and docked in New York on June 21, 1941. My dad rushed on board to find me, and helped me get my *Zamzam* bag and suitcase of accumulated clothing through customs. We had received instructions not to discuss our adventure with the press until we had met with the AIM mission executives. The press was all around us, taking pictures and plying us with questions. They overheard me babbling my story to my father, and I am afraid I gave them early headlines of the story. Suddenly, I was home and standing on American soil – concrete rather – embraced and kissed by my whole family and many friends from the church.

Alice, wearing her French beret and the same (now shrunken) suit in which she swam in the Atlantic, as she was about to board the liner Mouzinho in Lisbon, Portugal.

We missionaries from the *Zamzam* spent the night in New York so we could attend the mass celebration of our safe return by the AIM leaders and a number of other mission societies. They had not wanted the press to get the story from us, but from them. In an ironic twist, the AIM headquarters later sued the *Zamzam* line for our losses. After years of wrangling, I think I got a final settlement check for $300, which almost covered what I owed the Red Cross.

It would be an understatement to say that I was exhausted from my experience. I look back now and I realize that I should have rested and spent more time with my family. But,I had a fantastic story to tell and I was as excited to tell it as my many audiences were to hear it. I probably had an average of at least one speaking engagement a day for the next six months. My dad bought me a car so I could travel to speak to anyone who invited me. God had kept me and revealed His care and power to me through great danger. I felt honored to share my testimony of His providence with as many people as possible.

CHAPTER 4
Africa At Last

After the initial excitement of my return from the war zone in Europe, and after making the rounds to share my experience, I decided to go back to Moody Bible Institute to complete my diploma. America had just entered the war after Pearl Harbor in 1941, and it was extremely dangerous to cross the Atlantic by ship. I expected to have time to finish my semester at Moody, but I received a telegram from AIM headquarters in New York that a boat bound for Mombasa was accepting reservations. I had already had several false starts toward leaving and I did not want another. Besides, I had just a few weeks left in my final semester at Moody and I was to be class speaker.

I really had to know if leaving this time was the will of God. I began to pray diligently and one morning during my devotions, someone slipped a piece of paper under my door. On it was a note that said, "I read this and thought of you, Alice." The verse of Scripture on the paper was from Deuteronomy 10:11, which said, "Arise, proceed on your journey ahead of this people." I took that to mean that I should leave immediately, even before graduation. I asked God for a verse of final confirmation and got two—from Deuteronomy 11:26-28: "Behold, I am setting before you a blessing and a curse. A blessing if you obey, and curse if you do not." That seemed pretty clear to me.

I informed the dean of women of my decision not to finish my term. She encouraged me to call my pastor at Calvary Church to see if he would confirm the Lord's leadership. Dr. Torrey was warm and fully supported my decision to go immediately. So it was that I left Moody in Chicago and after a few days of farewell at home, found myself once again in New York, ready to sail across the Atlantic during full-scale war this time.

November 21, 1942, was cold and windy in New York. When we got to the old Egyptian liner, I had a stomach ache. I couldn't believe my eyes. The ship docked before me could have been the run-down twin of the *Zamzam*. As I arrived on deck after a somber goodbye to my family and friends from Calvary Church, I learned that it was, in fact, the sister ship to the *Zamzam*, named *El Nil*. The *Zamzam*'s name in Arabic was *El Misri*. The two were truly twins—the miserable nothings! A few weeks out in the ocean, we affectionately re-christened the *El Nil*, the "Ill Smell!"

I unpacked my suitcase in the cabin below, then came back on deck to wave goodbye as we loosed from the tug and slipped out of the harbor under a thick cloud of black smoke. I noted the dirty deck and the general untidy appearance of the ship as I lost sight of land. I can assure you that I paid close attention to the lifeboats, giving them an extra glance to be certain they were in working order. Perhaps the ill smell kept the Germans away – or perhaps, it was something else!

To my surprise and pleasure, there were other young, single missionaries bunking in my cabin. They were all bound for the Belgian Congo. I was delighted to have their happy company. Mary White and Jessie Blanchard were also nurses. They would serve in the Belgian Congo with AIM.

There was no rainbow this time, but we steamed very peacefully straight for South Africa for two weeks. We saw no other ships or debris from a sinking and felt relaxed – reading and taking tea on deck, all tucked in under our blankets. Frankly, I needed the rest.

It was sometime in the third week as we were close to the coast of South Africa that our captain informed all of us headed for East Africa that he was not going to stop in Mombasa, but sail up the coast to Eritrea. We could get off in Cape Town or in Aden. End of discussion!

His unilateral decision left a good number of us in a pickle. How were we to get from Cape Town, South Africa to Nairobi, Kenya? It was apparently none of his concern. Directly, without much ado, he put us ashore in Cape Town, then sailed north along the East African coast. He refused to refund us one penny of our unused ticket expenses.

We were totally unprepared for Cape Town. And frankly, Cape Town was completely unprepared for us. The rest of Africa must have been empty because it seemed like every living soul, at least the white ones, were milling around in this one city. It finally dawned on us that it was Christmas season, and soldiers and their families as well as the average white South African had come to the coast for the holidays. It took us all day to find a room in some missionary guest-house on the outskirts of town.

To our further surprise, we discovered that Cape Town was cold, for it was so far south of the equator it even snowed there on occasion. We buttoned up and soon settled in to enjoy the food, the beautiful city and the festive shops. We rode the sky-tram up Table Mountain and visited the museums and the zoo. There were no ships going to Mombasa—ever again, it appeared.

My friends were taking the gold train from Cape Town to Stanleyville (now Kisangani), the capital of the Belgian Congo at that time. They finally persuaded me to ride with them to the Congo and then figure out a way to get to Kenya from there. Cape Town men wiser than I reckoned that it could be done, but probably not by a single woman alone. I guess I thought I would be the first, so I decided to take the gold train with my friends. After the *Zamzam*, what could happen to discourage me? To make sure nothing did, I used the Cook Travel Agency in Cape Town to secure passage on the gold train, the lake steamers and the railroads that they assured me I would need to use to get to Kenya. I paid them, took their vouchers and headed off to the train station as if I were merely traveling in America. They made it sound straightforward.

The train I boarded was called a "gold" train, I soon learned, because it carried white mining executives and their treasure back and forth between the gold and diamond mines of the Congo and South Africa. Native miners rode a different train, naturally. The train could hardly be described as opulent, but it was comfortable enough. The conductor had the odd habit of stopping for every meal when we would get off and find some tea shop for a snack or pick up local fruit, which was abundant. We also stopped to take on water and wood for the steam engine. Our halting little caravan took a full three weeks to travel a thousand miles over the peaceful scenery of the stunningly beautiful landscape of Southern Africa. Apparently, it was quite all right to shoot game from the train, which would obligingly stop to retrieve – or, just as often, not.

Stanleyville, when we finally arrived there, was a vision of paradise. I was totally unprepared for the lush gardens and tidy, modern city in the middle of Africa. The town was named for the reporter, Henry Morton Stanley, who was sent to locate the eminent missionary doctor, David Livingstone. Suddenly, I found myself in a bustling European city, quite perplexed as to how to act and get around.

Fortunately, AIM had some missionaries posted there and I was able to stay with them. I enjoyed looking in on the leper work and the general clinic activities that the nurses and doctors allowed me to see.

The problem of how a single female might get to Kenya from Congo over land occupied the missionaries on many an evening. I prayed constantly for guidance, notwithstanding my Cook voucher book. It seemed that all the senior men could agree on was that the best plan would get me to Lake Tanganyika and from there, to Lake Victoria. But, the farther away from Stanleyville, the exact schedule and manner of travel I was to take became less clear. The rainy season would soon break, and it was imperative that one traveled during the dry season.

In a week, I secured passage on a river steamer that carried expatriates down the mighty Lualaba (Congo) River—one of the deepest in the world, reaching 700 feet in places. The steamer's crew recognized my Cook vouchers, to my amazement. It could be a treacherous river in the rainy season, they said, but they gladly booked me.

In February 1943, therefore, I boarded the steamer with six cabins – whites only to be sure. We each had a suite and the dining room was like a hotel. I was lucky to be befriended by a Mennonite family, who adopted me for the ride as far as Tanganyika (now Tanzania). We ate together and played games in the evening.

We set off for what was billed as a two-day jaunt to a remote port at the mouth of the river, where one of the headwaters of our river highway flowed out of Lake Tanganyika. It seemed odd that we were steaming against the current, but this ancient, dirty river had its origins in streams high in the uncharted mountains of several distant countries.

On the second day, I finished my breakfast and devotions, and then went on deck to get some warm sunshine and observe what I hoped would be lush landscape teeming with game. We chugged our way up the middle of this deep, dirty river. The entire time I stood on the deck, I saw only one herd of elephants coming down to drink. Mile after mile of plantation passed before my disbelieving eyes. Cocoa, rubber, bananas, citrus, coffee, tea, sisal and other vegetation in neat rows slipped silently by. Not what I had expected of the African jungle!

As I stood there in obvious surprise, my Mennonite friend sidled up to the rail. He explained to me that the Belgians "owned" this country and that the natives were virtually slaves in their own homeland. It was nothing short of amazing what slave labor had produced! My hometown had a chocolate factory, I recalled. Its supply of cocoa may have come from these very slave plantations. I learned later that U.S. chocolate comes from plantations on the West Coast of Africa, but chocolate never quite tasted the same after that brief introduction to its cultivation.

As we steamed toward Lake Tanganyika, the scenery changed to less developed highlands and forests. The rains broke and fell in torrents in the afternoon. We were happy to take our tea in the warm, plush lounge as the rain soaked the decks and washed the windows. Finally, one morning, in bright sunshine, the vessel docked at a ramshackle pier and jetty. We tied up and porters put my things on the boardwalk. We were still in the Belgian Congo, apparently in the lake town of Kalemie, where Lake Tanganyika emptied into what turned out to be the Lukuga River, a major tributary of the Lualaba. The British, however, seemed to be running the place. I would catch the British lake steamer here and head for Kigoma, Tanganyika.

Lake Tanganyika was under British colonial authority at that time, and it was a gruff, out-of-sorts Englishman who greeted us and marched us through his fenced customs area. Since we had no weapons or contraband to declare, we were let out of the gate in order to wait for a lift to the lake steamer that would take me on the next leg. My Mennonite family friends bade me farewell, and I was alone. And, I felt alone for the first time. There I was, right in the very middle of darkest Africa! I was not afraid, however, for the verse from Psalm 23 gave me confidence: "Yeah though I pass through the valley of the shadow of death, I will fear no evil for thou art with me. Thy rod and Thy staff, they comfort me."

Fortunately, the lake steamer was already tied up at the dock, so I handed over another voucher and boarded it immediately. This craft was not at all of the size or shape of the first one, nor was it segregated. We had to spend one more night in port waiting for some passengers, but the next day we would set off for a town called Kigoma, way up on the northeast shore of this the largest of the jeweled lakes that adorn the neck of the Albertine Rift Valley. There I hoped, I could catch the passenger train for Lake Victoria.

The next day, I set sail again. Uniformed African sailors untied the tiny steamer, filled to the gunwales with produce and natives. There was the odd English administrator aboard, but they kept to themselves as we plied our way north to Kigoma for another day on a freshwater lake rimmed in the distance by thickly forested mountains. Thankfully, it did not rain on us, and I could sit on the deck all day watching the water birds and African shore life when we put in to pick up passengers.

We docked at Kigoma, and my belongings were taken off and loaded onto a vehicle driven by a missionary who had somehow been alerted that I was arriving. The next morning, I booked a ticket on the East African Railroad on Her Majesty's Service, a passenger train that would eventually get me to Mwanza on the southern tip of Lake Victoria.

With a day to myself, I took a side trip to the burial ground of the famous Dr. Livingstone at Ujiji, a stone's throw south of Kigoma. It was pretty much unimpressive and dirty, but I suppose it was preserved just as it had been when he was buried there in 1873.

The next morning, I took the train out of Kigoma for Mwanza. The British, and the Germans before them, had done an amazing feat of engineering to get a railroad across so many rivers that all flooded with rainfall rushing down from high in the hills to gather into raging rivers that emptied into Lake Victoria. Lake Victoria is itself a huge reservoir (the largest freshwater lake in the world), which, when it fills with seasonal rain, empties through a narrow gorge at Owens Falls and forms one of the arms of the Nile that meanders through Sudan all the way to Egypt. The scenery crossing those trestles was spectacular and lush. There were surprisingly few villages along the route, although there were settlements where we stopped for meals and fuel.

The train was slow climbing up and down those mountains, and we took more time than I had expected getting to Mwanza. We finally arrived and once again, missionaries met me and offered lodging until I could book the next leg of my journey. Only one lake steamer made the rounds of the four largest ports, and it took a week for it to get all the way around the huge lake. Having just missed it, I had a week of time on my hands. I stayed at an AIM guesthouse run by a jolly elderly couple. The food was fresh and tasty, and each day I went out to observe the rural medical clinics in preparation for what I would be doing when I eventually got to Kenya.

The lake steamer I boarded at the end of my week in Mwanza plied the growing ports of Lake Victoria. It was run by the British and ferried a great deal of goods and people around the lake. It was a seaworthy vessel with several decks. I had my own berth, but I spent much of the time on deck watching the fishermen among the little islands we passed by. From time to time, a massive thunderhead formed in the distance to drop its cold rain in slatey shafts fractured by forked lightning. The distant thunder was awesome and as I watched, I could only call to mind, the Scripture that my Heavenly Father's voice was like thunder and His tongue like a flash of lightning. Here before me was a display of the massive power of my Creator. Thankfully, we never went through one of those famous Lake Victoria storms that could swamp a lesser ship. I was simply content to watch the storms in the distance – happy not to live through one or to contemplate another sinking.

We steamed all day and all night straight across the great lake and put into the port of Kisumu, Kenya, the next morning. Again, missionaries met me and took me and my belongings directly to the train station. My Cook travel voucher worked again, and I found my sleeping car—this was a proper British passenger train—and settled in for a night of thump-thump, thump-thump down the darkened Great Rift Valley, past the volcanoes of Suswa and Longonot on the escarpment at 7,000 feet altitude down onto the sprawling, sun-drenched Athi Plains and into the booming town of Nairobi, the capital city of Kenya. I slept through it all.

It was March 8, 1943, when I awoke the next day in Nairobi. More than three months had passed since I had left New York. I was tired and excited and a bit confused. What to do now? I stood there on the red-ochre-stained concrete platform with my cases trying to get my bearings when a vaguely familiar voice called out to me. I turned and there was John Schellenberg, the man I had sung a duet with in New York almost two years ago. He cheerfully offered me his hand. Beside him was AIM Field Director, Dr. Elwood Davis.

They quickly loaded me and my baggage into the director's handsome vehicle and chugged off to the AIM rest home – affectionately known to all as Mayfield. This cut-stone, colonial home converted into apartments was to become my home for a few weeks as I settled in to life in the British colony of Kenya. Elspeth Huxley had already immortalized colonial life in this paradise which she had called "White Man's Country". I had to register with the American consulate, which John helped me do. I also had to sign up for language training at the government language school. John knew this place well as he had just passed his government language test in Kiswahili.

Word came to me that I was temporarily assigned to the large mission hospital high up on the escarpment of the Great Rift Valley, with a view of the volcanoes I had passed in the night. Quite happily, John informed me that he, too, was going to Kijabe to take a month's vacation, which he was due for having passed his language exam. He borrowed an old Model T Ford and we set off up the dusty road along the escarpment of the Great Rift Valley to Kijabe. The view and the elevation were both breathtaking. My heart was racing.

John found lodging with a young missionary couple and I stayed at the guest room for visiting medical types. I was scheduled to observe and then assist the one expatriate staff RN at the hospital. She would come into the hospital at about 9 a.m. then leave for lunch and not return. I was confused since I needed all the orientation and experience I could get. There was nothing to do about it, and I dared not complain about my situation to anyone.

The one bright spot in the entire episode was that every evening, a different couple from around the station would invite John and me to dinner. We became an "item" at Kijabe, and everyone expected us to be engaged shortly.

We spent our month happily together and enjoyed our fellowship with the other missionaries. I got little from my nursing experience, but I took that as the pace of Africa to which I must adjust.

We were one day from packing up and heading back to Nairobi. Field Council would be meeting to assign me a station and a clinic, as well as language study. I was looking forward to getting down to serious work.

That night, the moon was full and unusually bright – perhaps because of the thin air of Kijabe. The wind sighed through the tall wattle and eucalyptus trees that cast their dancing shadows on the hard dirt road around us as John escorted me home from dinner. He refused to touch me, but I fully expected him to propose that night. It was his last chance and the stage was perfectly set. There is nothing like the romance of an African full moon!

John finally stopped, touched my elbow gently, and asked me to stop and look at him. I turned to look up at his smiling face and he asked me if I would marry him, declaring his "undying" love. The problem was that, as much as I liked him, enjoyed his company and trusted him completely, I was not ready to get married just then. I felt like I had to get my assignment and language training first. The Lord had, after all, called me to be a nurse.

The last thing I wanted to do at that moment was hurt him, but I had to tell the truth. So, I took his arm, looked into his moonlit face and told him gently that I could not say "yes" at that time. I did not tell him that I did not yet love him like I wanted to love the man I married. I simply stated that I liked him, but I was not ready to marry him right then.

He turned away without a word, and we walked silently to my apartment where he said good night. I went to bed in great turmoil over what had just happened. But, I consoled myself with the fact that I had no leadership from the Lord in the matter of marriage to John and without it, I was not making a lifetime commitment that would override the one I had already made to my Lord.

I had it settled in my mind, but the sadness on John's face as we drove silently back to Nairobi the next morning was hard to bear. Neither of us made any mention of the failed proposal. The trip took forever, it seemed to me. When we got back to Mayfield, we both put on a brave public face and went about our business – I organized my medicines as directed by Field Council and John got ready to return to his assigned station, Mulango, in the malaria-infested lowlands of Kitui in the dry, eastern scrubland that skirts the Yatta Plateau.

I did step out to wave goodbye to him the next morning as he set off. Then, I turned my heart to language study.

CHAPTER 5
The Home of the Buffalo

The AIM Field Council met in July 1943 and assigned me to go to Mbooni, to both study the Kikamba language and to fill in the position of nurse at the station clinic. Mbooni was in the eastern province of Kenya, which was tribal land of the third-largest Bantu tribe, the Akamba. The nurse who had been at Mbooni station for many years had recently died and there was no government clinic within twenty miles. I was to replace her, and I couldn't wait to get there.

While I was thrilled to have an assignment in Ukambani, the tribe where John worked, my station would be some ninety miles from his and over 2,000 feet in elevation above his. Mbooni was a lush paradise compared to Kitui, where John lived. Mbooni means "the home of the buffalo," and so it once was – a wild mountain, thickly forested and thinly populated. By the time I got there, the buffalo were long gone and in their place, thousands of villages with their mud and grass-thatched huts clung to the steep hillsides, slowly being denuded. The fires of witchcraft and wild, traditional drumming still filled the night even though missionaries had lived there since before the turn of the century.

The British had already begun major terracing on the mountain slopes to stop erosion and promote the cultivation of intense, irrigated vegetables and fruit. The recently restored forests on the ridge encouraged rainfall, and this water ran down the mountain continuously to be diverted into ditches that watered vegetables and every conceivable variety of fruit.

The day came when I packed my belongings in Nairobi and rode to Mbooni via Machakos with George Weppler. He and his wife had lived at Mbooni Station for decades and both knew the language fluently. Their children had already graduated from the AIM boarding school at Kijabe, the now famous Rift Valley Academy, and were back in America. I stayed in a spare room in their home, which was a massive, old German-built bungalow with thick mud walls and a corrugated-tin roof from which came all of our drinking water—never mind that the tanks were seamed with toxic lead at that time. The yard was covered with thick grass and dotted with numerous, mature fruit trees, laden with custard apples, oranges, tangerines and even apples. Someone, a colonial builder, had even put in a proper tennis court.

My first meal in the Wepplers' delightful home remains indelible in my mind. I took a warm bath in a tin tub that first evening after sundown, dressing with my sweater around my shoulders as it got cold at 6,000 feet after dark. We sat down around a mahogany table and chairs. The table was draped with an exquisite, lace tablecloth that glowed a warm ivory in the light of a kerosene lamp on a wooden stand by the head of the table. After a pleasant grace, Mrs. Weppler shook a tiny brass bell; a barefoot African man, clothed in a white robe with a dark red fez on his head, pattered into the dining room, bowed and said only, "*Memsaab?*"

She spoke to him in muffled Kikamba as she ordered the first course. He went away and returned carrying a tray with a china tourine of soup, which he ladled out into china bowls on the sideboard and then set them properly before us. The next course was fresh poached fish with mixed vegetables in butter. The "boy" (as they were called in those colonial times) cleared the fish plates and then brought in polished, warm dinner plates onto which he served our entrée. In a moment, he was back to pour water, bowed and slipped back to the kitchen with the swish of his white, starched *kanzu* robe to await the next bell. The meal (and so many like it that followed in the next months) grew into a true colonial banquet.

We took our demitasse coffee in tiny, opaque china cups in the drawing room in front of a great fire. Altogether, it was a stunning and entirely satisfying repast. As it turned out, that was how it was done—not just on the occasion of my arrival, but almost every day. How glad I was for my silver service and china on its way from Nairobi. We didn't dine like that every day, but when we had important guests, we could and did.

The very next day, I ventured down to the low, whitewashed clinic with its tin roof for my first day as a nurse in Africa. I passed a green, tin water tank and one greasy, wooden bench on the front veranda – already half filled with sick villagers who had somehow heard that *muiiti*, the nurse, had returned.

A wave of Dettol disinfectant washed over my face as I opened the door. Two native "dressers" in white stood in the empty room by a table and bowed to greet me in English. They were government-trained and surprisingly knowledgeable. I insisted on speaking only Kikamba, as I believed immersion in the language would speed up my command of it. I had already learned a few medical phrases to begin with, but they proved little help as, right away, the sick jabbered at me as if I knew what they were saying.

I looked around, and all I could see were a few neat rows of brown bottles and some open boxes of bandages on the shelves. That was it for medicine or for anything else, except for a table and chair and a well-worn log book in the next room. My dressers did not know what the liquid in any bottle might be, but they told me what they would use it for. I inquired as to how the former nurse knew what she was administering, and was very surprised to see them pour a few drops on the backs of their hands and lick it. She knew by taste.

I had, fortunately, brought up a box of labeled drugs and proceeded to destroy the entire stock of odd bottles on the shelves. Down the pit latrine they went with a tinkle and a sucking in of breath by the two dressers, who must have reckoned that their entire stock of "magic" potions was now lost. It was wartime and drugs were hard to come by, so I had only something to treat malaria, some gentian violet and mercura-chrome for the rash of cuts and foot sores I saw every day. My biggest and most common problems, however, were with pregnant women and their nursing babies. I learned the Kikamba word for diarrhea before any others.

That first day fairly flew by, and I dragged my tired body up the hill past the fruit trees in the purple, African dusk, praying that no black mambas or red cobras were lying in wait for me in the bamboo thicket that grew along the path. The workmen killed at least one of those terrible snakes almost every week for the first year I lived at Mbooni. Oddly enough, I rarely saw any snake-bite victims at the clinic. That was a good thing because, as for anti-venom, there was none.

I settled into a routine and enjoyed learning the language under the difficult but real conditions of its daily use. Mrs. Weppler and a local woman taught me formal grammar and speech. Rose Horton, a senior single missionary who was translating the Bible into Kikamba, also took a turn at inculcating the more difficult theological terms into my farm-girl head. We always took tea in the afternoon, and I tried to run through the dozens of patients that lined up in the clinic yard by teatime. I shared in the cooking and learned to present a formal five-course dinner myself. Occasionally, we had British government officials come through and such occasions were a high point for entertaining.

Mrs. Weppler never tired of telling her guests that the doors, windows and lovely, leaded glass on her china cabinet had been ported by natives on their heads all the way from Mombasa some 200 miles to the east and had come from America before that. The original builder of the house was a Bwana Rhodes (pronounced "Lozy", since the Kamba cannot say their R's) was the first American missionary on the hill. He was somehow related to Cecil Rhodes, for whom Rhodesia was named.

He had paid the Kamba villagers all along the twisting, treacherous slopes up the mountain to dig the roadbed for him for one penny a day. They did so only because the colonial administration required every native to be counted and to pay a head tax (called a poll tax) as well as a hut tax in sterling. This worked very well to provide those who needed it with labor and those who labored with the necessary tax money – and no more, it should be noted. Industrious natives could earn more money by selling food to the growing towns of Machakos and Nairobi, once they had their land terraced and irrigated – and once they had paid their taxes.

During the rainy season, the muddy main road to Mbooni from Machakos that wound around sheer gorges and crossed deep, sandy river beds was all but impassable. I had to stock up on drugs, firewood and food for the rainy season that very predictably came twice a year – in late October and again in March. I busied myself with records and letter-writing during those cloudy, rainy seasons on the mountain.

John in Kitui was someone with whom I had continued to correspond, and when a mail carrier could get down to Machakos, the district headquarters, I could get his letters after only a few weeks delay – which, of course, was when he got mine.

He wanted to come and see me, he wrote one day after my first two months at Mbooni. I looked forward to that and told him so. He would love the lush, green hillsides and fantastic food of this place.

I put thoughts of John working in dry, dusty Kitui out of my mind and went about my duties in my private paradise. One Friday morning, a lady came to the clinic carrying a beautiful clay pot, which she promptly told me in Kikamba was for me, now that I was "one of them." A dresser whispered to me that this was the famous Syo Myove, the very first woman to become a Christian on Mbooni hill. She smiled and untied the sisal rope holding the pot on her head and gently set the orange-colored clay pot on the cement floor. She bent over and struck the pot with her index finger. It rang like a bell. She straightened with a sly smile and told me proudly that it was the best. She had made it just for me!

Syo Myove (pronounced "Syoh Me-yo-veh") had become a famous and increasingly wealthy woman from making excellent pots out of the rich, red clay of Mbooni hill. The next day was Saturday, and she promised to come around to the mission house in the afternoon and escort me to her home to teach me how to make pots. I wanted to hear her amazing story accurately, so I made a note to bring along a translator. She was not needed, however, because Syo Myove's children spoke English perfectly well.

After I took my lunch and had a short nap, the houseboy came to inform me that Syo Myove was sitting outside waiting for me. I went to meet her with my purse and hat, and a large umbrella. One must not sit in the tropical sun too long. She stood up, stopped knotting her half-done sisal basket that she had been all the while weaving patiently, and shook my hand. She was a slight woman, not old but wrinkled already, with deep-set, twinkling eyes. She put her small hand into her pocket and pulled out three brown chicken eggs. For me! I protested that Kamba women did not eat eggs. She corrected me with a giggle to say that white women did.

She took my hand and escorted me from the mission compound along a path that led slightly down the hill shaded by massive eucalyptus trees, whose jagged, gray roots grew like claws down each bare slope holding the precious soil in place against the force of erosion. She found her footing and then took up her basket weaving as we walked. I was dumbfounded at her skill, for she never missed a count while walking and talking! It was nothing, she remarked. She would usually be carrying water and firewood while she wove her sisal baskets.

The bare clay of the cut-along the path was pink and ochre with streaks of mica that sparkled in the dappled sunlight. I could hear the sounds of voices echoing up the hill as the path turned steeply down and into a grove of wattle trees, obviously planted for harvesting in a few years. She told me that she grew the trees for their bark, which white men from Thika came to buy to tan their animal hides. The Kamba used the supple trunks for weaving the framework on which to thatch their huts.

The clay along the path turned to a dark, brick red and I noticed huge-cave-like excavations as we neared her village. Men were stomping up and down in one such cutaway into the steep hillside to make mud, which they threw into wooden forms to make adobe brick. She would show me how to make a clay pot in due time, she insisted, but first I had to sit and drink the customary cup of bush tea.

A folding chair was brought for me, and my friend sat on her three-legged stool and smiled. We chatted politely as her children set a small table and brought an enamel pot of more tea and hard-boiled eggs for the white lady. Our ritual meal of friendship over, she began to narrate the story of her conversion to Christianity.

After the colonial adventurer, the famous Mr. Lozy, had built the place and left, the Wepplers had settled in. Syo Myove, a young, newly married, fifteen-year-old, became very curious to know why the whites had come and what their culture was like. Wherein lay their seemingly great power? She spent days hidden in the hedge watching and listening. She went to the clinic to learn white healing practices. In due course, she made up her mind that these were not only harmless folk, but good people who came to help her tribe. Many Africans did not differentiate between missionaries and colonials, but she did.

Against all advice from her husband and family, she went one day to visit Mrs. Weppler, who greeted her kindly and offered her tea on the veranda. Syo Myove inquired of her as to the reason for her being there and what she was doing—her work. She also wanted to know how to make a dress like the white lady's. The colors were beautiful and the feel of the cloth was wonderful. When Mrs. Weppler explained the Gospel to her and what it meant to be a Christian, Syo Myove gave her heart to Jesus and in a short time was baptized—the first married woman to be converted and join the newly constructed church just down the hill from the clinic.

Syo Myove was overjoyed to receive her first communion with her family crowded around the windows on the outside to watch that fateful service. When she came out, a humiliated and enraged husband dragged her to his hut, stripped her dress off and beat her till she could not stand up. She said nothing to him and refused to cry, she told me. It was his duty to defend his honor and hers to endure his violence in doing so. She could endure this suffering for her Savior's sake.

Alice went back shortly after her first retirement to visit her old friends at Mbooni, Syo Myove and Syo Mbole. Here she poses with Syo Mbole.

No one was allowed to tend to her or call the white nurse. She mended enough to go to church again the next Sunday, but another beating followed. She told me then that she feared her angry husband would beat her to death. She could not go to the white missionaries with her story or she would be killed for sure.

Syo Myove then did a brave thing. She ran away into the forest as far as she could run and then, exhausted, fell to the ground, weeping. In her distraught state, she cried out to her newfound Jesus and begged for guidance for what to do, what to eat and where to seek shelter. She was alone, but somehow not frightened. She waited for God to speak to her.

She said she heard a voice as she prayed on her knees in the damp forest. I have given you all you need, it said. She asked God not to mock her in her sorrow and asked what He meant by those words. You are kneeling on strong red clay, my gift. Mix it with your tears and this clay will be a clear sign that I am the true God for your people. You will be a potter.

Syo Myove somehow survived those difficult days in the forest, building a shelter, digging up roots, and eating small hyrax in the rocks she caught and cooked. She began to mix clay and learned to make coils of it and fire them. She told me that she learned pottery from the hand of the Master Potter. It was the same potter who had made her, she had discovered from the Bible. She would be the best. In fact, for years, she was the only potter. No African on the hill doubted that the pots she made were a miracle. She had never seen a pot made nor was she of the pot-making clan. However, seeing a miracle does not make everyone believe in God!

She stood up midway through her story and motioned for me to come to her pottery pit, where she made her pots, so I could see how she did it. Her children were there apprenticing to be potters after her. She showed me how she wound long coils of perfectly smooth clay into the wide bottom half of a pot. Then, she made the top with its narrowed neck in much the same way. To my surprise, the two halves fit together perfectly. She set the finished pot down on fresh banana leaves to cure. Later, it would be fired in a kiln and turn a deep orange – her trademark.

We went back to sit down so she could tell me the rest of her story. It seems that she sold her first cooking pot in the local market for one shilling—a great deal at that time. It was still cheaper than pots imported from the western province of Kenya. She took that shilling and went to buy a shirt from Mrs. Weppler. This she gave to her husband. He liked it, but he nevertheless refused to let her move back into her hut at his compound. Undeterred, she continued to pray for him, to bring him gifts and clothes for the children. When he was drunk on local beer, he would catch her and beat her – to remind her that she was still his wife! She worked patiently and soon became quite wealthy and well known on the hill. She studied the Bible and went to catechism with Mrs. Weppler.

Alone in her hut one day, God spoke to her, Syo Myove told me. He told her that a great famine was coming to Ukambani and even to Mbooni hill. She must prepare for this and help her people. She must stop making pots and plant sweet potatoes, God told her. But she did not know what sweet potatoes were then. God instructed her to go to the Wepplers who grew them. The Wepplers gladly showed her what they were and how to start many vines from small cuttings.

Syo Myove grew many hundreds of slips from those first tubers and then, without really knowing what she was doing, buried them everywhere she could in the forest clearings. Just as predicted, in a few years, a severe drought came over Kenya, and the traditional maize and beans failed completely. There was no food to eat and what they did grow, they had to sell for cash. As if that was not bad enough, that year there was also a plague of locusts that came down from Somalia and Sudan. These hordes of insects were so thick that they darkened the sun and made such an eerie sound as they consumed every living thing in their path—tree leaves, tomatoes vines and corn stalks. There was nothing green left above ground after they moved on. Her sweet-potato vines were gone, but the nutritious potatoes lay buried just beneath the surface.

Many, many people and their cattle died that season, she told me sadly. God ordered her to go into the forest and dig up the tubers she had planted and teach her people how to cook and eat them. The Kamba had never seen a sweet potato before that time. There were many who feared this food from the white man. Maybe it contained magic that would kill or sterilize them. Syo Myove ate sweet potatoes in public every day and gave them to anyone who was starving. They were not for sale, even though she could have become a very rich and powerful woman – holding the key to life and death.

The sweet potatoes were a gift from God to her people, she told me finally. Her husband even ate them and then he, too, gave his heart to Jesus and invited her back. She decided to go back to him because she trusted the love of God to change him. It did change him and hundreds of others who had no doubt that God had saved them with His sweet potatoes.

To this day, her story reminds me of how important it is to obey the prompting of the spirit of God in our hearts, however foolish it may seem at the time. I surely rededicated my life sitting there on Mbooni hill with this wise woman – a vessel in God's hand from which poured forth love, kindness and beauty.

I went back to the mission compound from that visit humbled and completely committed to service that would manifest the love of God in my everyday life. How glad I was that I could give medical treatment to so many who had so little. My heart was as full as my days.

Then one day, a letter from John arrived. It was a month late, to be sure, but I opened it with some excitement to read that he had requested permission to come to Mbooni for a weekend visit. And, he would be arriving in one week! My heart skipped a beat and I rushed up the hill to ask the Weppler's what was going on. They laughed and said John was coming, and they had wanted it to be a surprise. They got that part right!

So, John was coming to see me on Friday in one week and for a whole weekend. What would we do? What would we eat? Where would he stay? What did he want? That whole week, my mind was in a whirl. Fortunately, George Weppler had begun to remodel the old house the first nurse had lived in, and he hung a door on a room with a fireplace so that John could sleep there. Mrs. Weppler had laid in plenty of food and was busy with her pastries. It seemed I was the only one un-prepared, but I went to work and prayed – excited, yet unsure of myself.

On Wednesday that week, I was buried under an unusual load of sick folks when my dresser came to me and tapped my shoulder. "*Bibi*," (which is to say," Miss"), he said, there was a white man riding up the hill on a bicycle, and he was sure it wasn't a government official. I threw off my apron and rushed to the door to see a smiling, dusty man with his pith helmet on pedaling up to my door. It was John and he was a full two days too early!

He hopped off his bicycle and rang the bell as he saw me. "*Hodi*," is all I remember him saying. That was the traditional way of greeting a home and asking for permission to enter. "*Karibu*," I replied, "Come in." We laughed and shook hands. It wouldn't do to show too much affection in front of the local people. I sent him up to the mission house to wash and rest and drink some tea

John and his trusty bicycle, which he rode far and wide in the war years, eventually pedaling some 90 miles to propose to his bride, Alice.

while I closed the clinic for the day and sent all but the worst cases home. Word of his early arrival would have instantly reached the mission house and Mrs. Weppler. George and his wife, Claudia, served us lunch and spent the day chaperoning us in their well-appointed home. I was tired and an afternoon break in such happy company was a tonic.

Early the next morning, before John showed up for breakfast, I was somewhat in a tizzy about what to do with him while I did my rounds at the clinic. Claudia proved more level-headed and said I should put him to work. John was a good carpenter, so I got him to make me some shelves and then a pair of nice benches with wood left over from the church construction.

On Saturday, we all prepared for a formal dinner with the district officer who lived up the hill. He would come around to meet John and catch us up on local politics and projects—a nice diversion and a perfect opportunity to display American hospitality to a British officer. We enjoyed a sumptuous dinner and then took our coffee in the sitting room before a roaring fire. Our British officer guest excused himself after the required leave-taking and then, to my surprise, so did the Wepplers. I abruptly said good-night to John, and he went to his room next door.

The next day, all four of us went to a remote church service, and it began to rain on our way home. I was soaked and freezing cold. We slithered home and finally warmed up in front of that great fire that one never lets completely die out during the rainy season. After tea and a light supper, the Wepplers again took their leave early in the evening. That left John and me alone by the roaring fire. This time, I did not leave.

Alone on a comfortable couch in front of a warm and lazy fire, I was feeling more secure about being close to John. The odd piece of eucalyptus wood sent its blue and orange flames and showers of sparks up the chimney like fireworks. The dancing fire conveniently occupied our thoughts for a time and the crackling sparks filled the silence between our awkward sentences.

Finally, John found the courage to realize the one moment that had given him the strength to ride ninety miles uphill on his bicycle to be with me. He turned to me and smiled. The orange firelight warmed his smiling face and my heart melted. I knew what he would say next. He actually got down on one knee, declared his love for me and then asked me so sweetly to marry him. I had no doubts whatsoever this time, so I said, "yes!" I knew it was the right thing to say.

It was done. We were engaged to be married. He promised me that he would return with haste to bring me a diamond ring. I loved him for it, but didn't expect him to find such a thing in Nairobi during the war.

My life, my work and my mission would never be the same. I trusted the Lord to guide me in this new direction for my life just as I had trusted Him in the past. It was His will, I knew with certainty. John just sat there holding me in his arms and staring at the fire for a long time. Our two shadows moved apart, and then together as we shared a slow and dreamy dance of love. It was early in the morning when the fire died out, and John took his leave to go to his house and I to my room. There was no chance I would go to sleep, as tired as I felt. I was getting married!

Early the next morning, John climbed on his bicycle and started what would be a much hastier ride down the hill through the thorn scrub to Kitui. I waved till he was out of sight, then went to open the clinic and treat the extra-long line of patients waiting for their nurse in silence. I can remember wondering what it must be like for one of those women to get married. Would they share my joy? Would they know love? Would my being there make a difference in their lives?

CHAPTER 6
Marriage, Mambas and Malaria

John and I soon discovered that we had to have permission from the Field Council to get married, so we met in Nairobi to ask their blessing and learn of our new assignment as a married couple. It was there that John produced a tiny – but oh, so brilliant – diamond ring and put it on my finger. What a fervent, romantic man he was! I never thought he would find a diamond during the war years, but apparently the diamond mines of Tanganyika had recently opened and diamonds became available in Nairobi just in time.

Dear Mrs. Weppler did not have as much energy for helping me plan the big day as I needed. I was so grateful, therefore, for the help from my bridesmaid in Machakos, what with a full clinic and no time to get to Nairobi to order shoes and a dress and flowers. But, we finally got it all done, right down to printed invitations and the obligatory public notice in the *East African Standard* newspaper in Nairobi.

Our wedding day dawned clear and warm. I had my dress and the bridesmaid's dress made from a pattern I had brought from America by an Indian tailor in Machakos. They fit perfectly, to my surprise. Machakos station friends had spent several days arranging the reception dinner for the afternoon before John and I would leave for a short honeymoon. Friends from Mulango carried the chicken dinner to Machakos on the big day. My flowers were delivered in miraculous condition from Nairobi that very morning. The men arrived by car—the officiating minister, who was our field director, then John and his best man, George Weppler.

On October 23, 1943, the Machakos AIM church was filled to the brim with Africans, no doubt curious about a white man's wedding. About fifty missionaries had made the trip to share in our nuptials, and they sat in the front row as honored guests. My bridesmaid was a young Canadian missionary, Hazel, soon to be married herself to a British missionary, Ken Phillips. I don't remember the long ceremony or even my vows today. I just remember putting on our rings, kissing John with joy and then sitting down to a feast that surprised even me, given the fact of war rations and the cost to put it on.

John and I left with a few gifts, mostly from the local Indian businessmen who appreciated our weekly orders of groceries and hardware from their shops. Having eaten, we changed into safari clothes, jumped into his

John and Alice at Machakos Station with their wedding party and friends. John's best man was George Weppler and Alice's bridesmaid was Hazel Phillips.

ramshackle Model T with noisy tin cans tied to the back bumper and sped off into the dust to our appointed honeymoon retreat.

It so happened that a Scottish, Christian sea captain named Sherston owned a large land holding nearby. It had been given to him for his commission in the British navy. On it, he built a luxurious bungalow. It was our good fortune that the Mission had an arrangement with him for missionaries to reserve it whenever he was away on duty.

It was to this retreat that the Model T found its way that afternoon. We had one full week alone on a lush ranch with servants, good food, and plenty of game watching and hiking high in the hills that let us look out for miles over the shimmering Athi Plains to the dark, forest-crested Machakos and Mua Hills ranges and on to Nairobi in the distant haze. We needed to rest and since we were both unschooled in love, we were determined to take our time to learn what it meant to love each other in every dimension.

A dreamy week of learning love and sharing good food and conversation passed too quickly – as such times always seem to do – before we had to pack up and drive to Nairobi. I had passed my written language exam, but was allowed by Field Council to take the oral test after my honeymoon. We settled our married selves into Mayfield and John dropped me off for classes downtown each morning, I sat for the fateful test at the end of a refresher week.

I passed that test, and since I was now married and officially a full-time missionary, I was assigned to return to Kitui with John, my new husband. I was invited to meet the august body of men called the Field Council by myself before I left with John for Mulango mission station at Kitui.

Alice and John, a happy couple, set off in a borrowed car for their honeymoon.

They wanted to know how strong I felt and then gave me one very clear instruction. They told me that my orders were to take one full year to get to know my husband and forge a strong marriage. They wanted to hear nothing about nursing or other kinds of work for one full year. I was not to submit any reports of work done. I was dumbfounded and deeply moved! Could it be that they knew something I did not?

John had the old Model T packed and even tied boxes on to the outside. It must have been a comical sight to see us bounce out of Nairobi. The road conditions grew steadily worse and it amazes me to this day what punishment those old cars absorbed back then. John was a superb mechanic and took great pains to see that his vehicle was in top condition. Breaking down in the bush was always a dangerous, and sometimes fatal, event.

I rather enjoyed the trip, with the canvas top down and the slow drive through amazing landscapes with lots of game animals bounding across the road. We were protected against the tropical sun by our pith helmets, but not from the dust. We would stop for a drink and to clean up a bit, or eat a picnic on a rock or a riverbank. Using the bathroom in the bush was a constant source of laughter and figured centrally in any missionary repertoire of African adventure stories. The key to not being featured in any such story was to check the bushes for thorns and your clothes for ants. There were no public restrooms anywhere except those that were very public indeed.

We pulled into Kitui town that afternoon, signed into the British record books at the armed outpost and drove through the pole barricade to the salute of the uniformed African guard with his 303 Enfield rifle of WWI vintage on his shoulder. John wasn't so sure it would actually fire, but we didn't want to find out. I went to buy bread and rice and John rushed around looking for a jerry can of gasoline to get us home. Gas was more precious than gold in those years, and he came back empty-handed.

John knew we would not make it to the house if we pushed on with the empty tank. He trudged over to the only British officer he knew well and asked him to borrow some gas. The officer refused to give him gas, but agreed instead to tow us the remaining four miles to Mulango. He did pull us down the road in a cloud of dust, and finally untied our car from his after we coasted up to the veranda of a bungalow almost identical to the one at Mbooni. He then stepped back to us and asked if everything was quite all right. It was a rhetorical question, for he did not wait for us to answer before he said, "Right then, good evening," and turned to leave us in the twilight.

Our fellow missionaries, the Farnsworths, had just gotten back minutes before us from safari. They nevertheless invited us over for supper and had their help make up our beds. Tired as John must have been, he picked me up and carried me across the threshold of our new home on that first night in Mulango – not, however, before he checked for snakes. I was determined not to be the first to enter any room and have a black mamba land in my lap the first night.

There being no houseboy, no bath and no mambas to greet us, we just fell into bed. The next morning, I awoke under a mosquito net to the sound of John expressing his displeasure to the houseboy. I got up, put on a robe and found a chamber pot in which to relieve myself. The distant pit latrine, wherever it was, was not an option for me that first morning.

I brushed my long, dusty hair as best I could, put on my clothes and went out on the flag-stoned veranda of this, another old, German, mud-walled bungalow. John was reading his Bible with his feet up on the low wall around the veranda and as soon as I appeared, he called to the kitchen for tea and breakfast. This time, it was ready.

I wanted to eat on the veranda and take in all the sights and sounds, the strange birds and shy people who passed by that we watched through the kaleidoscope of the thick-scented Frangipani trees next to the house. My husband insisted that we had to eat properly in the dining room and there, breakfast was soon served. The soft, pink papaya fruit with lemon melted away all my ill will toward the servants from the night before. The wheat gruel with milk and a tin cup of strong coffee was all I needed to feel at home.

After lush, green Mbooni, Kitui was like the Sahara—hot, barren, dusty. Dry doesn't begin to describe the place. At least the thick mud walls of our bungalow kept the house cool, and I could rest in the afternoon heat. Everyone and everything took a siesta, it seemed.

Thus it was that life at Mulango stirred in the early morning and then again late in the afternoon after a rest. Nothing much moved in the heat of the noon-day sun—except the mambas. They move faster in the heat, and they are the fastest snakes in the world to start with! After the house was put in order, I put myself to work studying Kikamba under the stern tutelage of the senior missionary, Emma Farnsworth. I was under no illusion that she herself ran the station and "the work" even though her husband was, de facto, the station chairman. He traveled a great deal to outlying schools and churches, which he supervised on behalf of the mission and the British colonial government. Churches often shared a compound with AIM-sponsored primary schools.

Mrs. Farnsworth took it upon herself to encourage me to open the clinic (which she called a dispensary). She lobbied all the other station missionaries including my husband, John. It seemed she was determined to have a clinic on her station, and she was confused as to why I was reluctant to treat patients when I was a qualified nurse—the Field Council directive notwithstanding.

Her insistence became a sore spot between us, yet I continued to study under her direction. John and Mr. Farnsworth began to travel to oversee schools so John could help with the growing work. John's heart was not in school work, however, but in evangelism and pastor training. He longed to visit remote locations where few missionaries had ventured and where the people had not heard the Gospel.

It was a joy and something of a relief for me to get to go on some of John's safaris. Mrs. Farnsworth was reluctant to let me leave until she saw the value for my language learning. I would see the old Kamba customs and be immersed completely in their culture and language.

We packed up the Ford and set out for exotic places like Tharaka toward the coast and baobab country. Here, the people were so primitive that the women wore nothing except a short grass skirt and men walked about naked or covered with only a loincloth. We would pitch our heavy canvas tent and build a fire along a dry riverbed. At night, John used his car battery to power a projector and showed slides of America and told the Gospel story.

We went to bed under our mosquito nets with the glow of dying coals

On safari with the Farnsworths in two vehicles at a tented camp in the scrub thorn of eastern Kenya, circa 1943.

in the fire pit. There is nothing in the world like an African night. The stars do not just shine. They sparkle and dance in the millions, and the Milky Way illuminates the landscape until the great African moon rises and bathes the world in its silvery light.

It's hard to sleep under such beauty and mystery. It's even harder to sleep when the native drums start up, thumping away with yelling and whistles reverberating through the entire night. I always wondered how they could work so hard during the day and play so hard all night.

The people in these remote villages, Christian or not, were extremely generous and we never pulled away from a week's safari among them without gifts of food, fruit and curios – carved animals or three-legged stools and even fly whisks. The war years were hard on us nutritionally and we definitely benefited by the local contribution to our diet – especially after I awoke one morning to nausea and a suspicion that I was pregnant.

I was indeed pregnant. I knew this because, from day one, I was nauseated every morning and vomited daily for the whole nine months. In spite of this condition and against Field Council orders, I was finally persuaded to open the dispensary and treat the unending lines of sick people who

Alice in pith helmet prepares her supplies for a bush clinic while two local women carrying water in gourds look on.

showed up at the clinic door every morning. With the war still on, my stock of medicines was as simple as it was at Mbooni. I just did what I could with the little that I had.

The worst part about it all was that I soon contracted malaria myself. I worked hard to discharge all the sick before 4 p.m. because, at that appointed hour, I felt a fever come over me and I was truly too sick to nurse. Then, to compound matters, John caught cerebral malaria and would convulse from a spiked fever so severely that I wondered how he would survive. Without the afternoon rest hour and prayer, I doubt we would have.

We did get some relief and stayed in touch with good European doctors in Nairobi, a day's rattling safari away, because I needed good pre-natal care. John took the opportunity to obtain the latest malaria drugs, which allowed him to keep working. Nairobi was cool and the food plentiful. We rested there. I booked my birth room in the British Maia Carberry Hospital

While Alice ran a clinic, John preached to the men. Here a group of men are dwarfed by a giant baobab which provided shade by its branches and a bench with its roots while they listen to John speak.

just a few minutes' walk from Mayfield, the AIM guest house. We returned to Mulango laden with supplies and feeling revived.

The English doctor we had seen insisted that I return for my first delivery a week before term so that any complications could be managed. I did not relish the idea of driving a whole day in a bumpy car while in labor, so we agreed. In December, just before the rains broke, I knew the time was near. I began to pack my clothes and some things for the baby. I noticed that John did not pack a suitcase. I asked him why not.

He was ordered by the regional chairman on behalf of Mrs. Farnsworth (newly widowed) to drop me off in Nairobi and return that same day to be sure that the ladies on the station were not without a man at night. There would be no debate. He tucked me into Mayfield, said a brief farewell and sped back to Mulango. It was my good fortune that the couple in charge of Mayfield were medical types. He was an American doctor and she a nurse. I couldn't have had better care.

When my water finally broke on December 2, 1944, these two escorted me on foot to the hospital, checked me in and contacted the doctor. I remember noting how sunny and clean the wards were. The staff was all European and well trained. I went into full, hard labor that night and our first-born daughter, Joanne, was born the next morning. She weighed only four and one-half pounds, and the post-partum nurse took it upon herself to fatten up this child. I had no milk, so the nurse tried to fix the problem by forcing me to drink great amounts of fluids, but to no avail. The rule back then was that a mother and baby had to remain in the hospital for two weeks. There was a great deal for me to learn and no chances to take in those times.

At the end of two weeks, little Joanne began to run a fever. She would not eat and shivered constantly. The doctor did not know what it was or what to do. He did not believe babies could be born with malaria. Fortunately, her Daddy came and we took her to the mission hospital at Kijabe, where she was diagnosed with malaria. She got better immediately with proper medication.

The three of us returned to Mulango after a month of rest and good food, arriving late at night after a thankfully uneventful drive. I was exhausted and still not fully healed from a tear I had received during delivery. I did not want to get out of bed, so John brought Joanne to me with a bottle of formula supplied by the hospital.

Joanne and Dan in the arms of loving Lena who cared for them as if they were her own.

Mrs. Farnsworth, not having any children of her own, sent over a note early that very morning insisting that I had to treat the sick as usual. I handed the baby to an African woman John had hired to care for Joanne when I was treating patients in the dispensary. She was named Lena and I am certain she was an angel. I dressed in my whites, pinned on my hat and dragged my weary body to the dispensary. There must have been a hundred people sitting there waiting. I treated them all, skipped supper and collapsed into bed that evening – unaware that I had a baby crying next to me all night.

The next day, the houseboy came in a panic to fetch me from the clinic some fifty yards from the house. I had put Joanne in her pram and covered her with a mosquito net in the shade. Lena was off for the afternoon and I still had patients. I could see the pram and I thought it would be safe there. I was paralyzed with fear when I saw his face, for I new precisely what had panicked him. Good lad he was though, for there, bleeding on the ground, was the biggest black mamba I had seen yet. He had killed it while it was coiled around the wheels of the pram. He begged me never to leave the baby outside. I picked Joanne up, thanked God for her safety and vowed never to leave her unattended again.

I don't know how I got through that first year of medical work and mothering. We killed mambas often – as many as five one day. We did not even take a vacation. Thankfully, Joanne did get well and finally put on some weight, and so did I. The war was still on, but Kenya was growing and we soon had better medicine and food supplies sent down every week from Nairobi.

The highlight of those first few years in Kitui was our time on safari. I escaped from the clinic. John had made me a strong wooden chest with racks to hold my medicine. It unfolded and displayed all the contents, so it was easy to find what I was looking for. He preached and discipled his faithful pastors and showed his slides at night.

I am sure it was on one such safari that I became pregnant again. Our second child was due in January of 1946. As the time came for delivery, I still had to manage the clinic, but we had won the battle with malaria and I was stronger. Then in December 1945, to my surprise, my water broke. This child was coming early. I called John and we did some wash, ironed our clothes and packed the car for a day's trip to the hospital—if I could make it.

We bounced along the dirt road, up the Yatta Plateau and into Thika. It began to rain and got cold. I was sitting in a soaking-wet seat holding a one-year-old little girl in a blanket. We drove into Mayfield after supper in the dark only to discover that the place was packed. It was the Christmas holidays. There was no place for us to sleep or put down the baby. John remarked that he felt like Joseph. I did not exactly feel like Mary! We decided immediately that I would be deposited at the hospital and John would return to Mayfield to see if someone would let him and his tiny daughter stay in their room.

I walked into the delivery suite at Maia Carberry for the second time. This time, however, it was Christmas Eve and the doctor fully intended to get to his Christmas party. The nurses were occupied, and all I could do was to find a gurney on which to lie down. John fetched a blanket and then an aide wheeled me into to a dark delivery room.

John left me there and took Joanne back to Mayfield. A kind lady had taken pity on the two of them, and called around to several missionary families to ask if they could host John and Joanne. A couple that we did not know well finally agreed and at midnight on Christmas Eve, John and Joanne collapsed into bed.

I was not so lucky, for my labor pains were excruciating. The doctor was still determined to get to his Christmas party, so he ordered the nurse to sedate me. He left, but it didn't work. The baby was coming anyway. I was writhing in pain, but the thought of a drunk doctor doing the delivery motivated me to push hard so the nurse I trusted would be able to help me deliver this child before the doctor got back.

Just before noon on Christmas Day, 1945, our son, Daniel, was born. He weighed slightly over five pounds, but he was healthy and had good lungs! He looked huge compared to Joanne. The doctor showed up tired and disheveled, but he found everything in order. The circumcision could wait – I insisted! John and Joanne appeared after lunch and brought flowers. The post-partum nurse was a delight for two weeks, then it was time to drive home to Kitui. I still had no milk, but we did receive a good supply of formula, much to my surprise.

I knew what – or rather, who – awaited me on my return, but I was in

Just before furlough John and Alice posed with their first two small children, Joanne and Daniel, at their home in Kitui, Kenya.

better shape after Daniel's birth and of course, Lena would be there to love and care for my two babies now. I dressed for work the next day and life went back to a routine, as much as life with two infants can.

In a few months, it was time for us to return to America for our first, and much needed, furlough.

John handed over his work to a new missionary, Sheldon Folk, who would escort us to Nairobi and then use our car while we were gone.

We loaded up suitcases and a picnic with two small children seated on blankets in the back seat with me. Sheldon sat in front with his rifle between his knees. He was an avid hunter.

We had decided to leave a day early to be sure we did not have any reason to miss our airplane in Nairobi. All went well until about two hours outside of Thika town, when I noticed a wheel rolling down the ditch beside us. John laughed and said he thought the wheel must be ours. It was!

The axle had broken and the bearings were strewn along the roadside in the dust. We spent an hour collecting them, then John said farewell, put the axle on his shoulder and proceeded to start walking toward Thika. We all hoped a ride would come along. Walking was dangerous.

John had walked a few miles when out of the bush stepped a black African carrying a huge gun. He had a bandolier of bullets strung over his shoulder. He was apparently as stunned to see John as John was to see him. The man laughed and asked John if he was hunting lions. He assured John that, if he were not hunting them, they were hunting him. Then, he invited John to meet his boss, an English hunter, intent on killing a lion in the vicinity.

On seeing John with his axle, the hunter quickly surmised car trouble. Decently, he offered to go back to the car and took the whole lot of us to Thika to the famous Blue Post Hotel, where the sound of water rushing over the Chania Falls filled each room. After a snack and a bottle, the children and I went to bed – without a look at the falls. Sheldon with his gun had stayed with the vehicle and our stuff.

Although it was just at closing time, John drove with the English hunter to find a car-parts store in Thika town. Miraculously, an Indian kept his shop open and more amazingly than that, he had the parts John needed. With new axle and bearings in hand, John and his kind benefactor headed back to the car. It was soon dark, and the hunter trained his car lights on the missing front axle while John put it back together. Then, John and Sheldon drove to Thika. The white hunter disappeared into the night. He never did share his name nor would he accept any money for his time and expense. I believe the Lord wanted us to make our flight.

John picked up his sleepy family from the Blue Post and the entire crew finally chugged into Mayfield around midnight. Beds for us and a crib for Daniel were ready. In the morning, as the tropical sun rose in the window, tiny, jeweled birds dipped their scimitar bills into the flowers that filled the window boxes. Suddenly, the world seemed peaceful. The war had just ended.

In a few hours, we would be on our way, high in the sky like those birds, humming our way to the land of plenty.

CHAPTER 7
Paradise Lost and Regained

Our flight from London on Pan American World Airways landed in New York on a cold day in 1947. A building contractor from Lancaster with his roomy station wagon managed to get all of our suitcases and baby bags and the four of us into his warm car. I was pregnant with our third child and very uncomfortable during the ride home in the cramped back seat with the children.

We sped home to Lancaster, where he unloaded us in an apartment he had renovated for us one flight of stairs above his office. He was kind and generous and would not accept any rent for our time there. We learned later that he was the general contractor who had built the new Calvary Church sanctuary on Pleasure Road.

I found it extremely difficult to manage the steep stairs, and keeping the children safe on the second floor proved a full-time job. Fortunately, I did not have to do any nursing! We had to leave the children often at night when we were entertained, and then spoke and showed slides of our work in Africa. The church kindly continued to pay our support while we were on furlough, but we needed to raise money for our return passage and to re-outfit completely with new equipment, including a durable vehicle. Because of my discomfort and the stairs, John immediately began writing and calling his family in Manitoba, Canada, to see if we could visit them and speak in some churches to begin our Canadian deputation—otherwise known as fundraising.

It was a relief, then, when in April of 1947, John and I and two small children boarded a train bound for Altona, Manitoba. Spring had turned the leaves green in Lancaster, but the further north we traveled, the colder and grayer it got. After crossing the Canadian border, the snow was so deep that the train seemed to be traveling in a white tunnel. The bishop of the local Mennonite church met us at the station and drove us to his spacious, warm farmhouse, where we were introduced to our first sip of *pluma moose* – a milky, cooked-fruit concoction. Everyone, including John, spoke German. I felt like we had landed on another planet.

The next day, the Bishop took us to our new residence. We found a one-room, wooden house with windows boarded up and one door, that he used for storing surplus grain. He had fixed it up with a stove, a heater and a quilted partition in the middle of the large room so that we parents could sleep with some privacy. The outhouse was twenty feet away. Getting to it with the children in sub-zero weather would not register in my mind.

The cold was absolute. The snow had drifted as high as the top of the granary door. And, every time it snowed (which was often), John had to shovel a channel to the driveway. We were there to do deputation and raise money for our return, so we were obligated to get out and travel even though our tropical blood revolted against the numbing cold that the citizens of this place actually appeared to enjoy.

We could not take the children with us, so the bishop sent over his twenty-year-old daughter to watch them while we traveled. When we got back home late, she just curled up with the children till morning. I began to pester John to find us a more suitable place to stay, an apartment or something with central heat and plumbing – and a second room. It was time for my third delivery, and I could not endure the thought of a newborn in those stark, primitive conditions. We did not want to appear ungrateful, but our "house" was unfit for our family.

The problem with finding and renting a new place in Altona was that we had so little money. The way deputation worked in Canada among the Mennonites at that time was that John would speak and the churches would send in money to a central account in our name, but under the signature of the bishop. John could request money for certain expenses, but the bishop had total control. He would be insulted if we did not fully appreciate his hospitality and respect his authority. He did finally see the need for more space. I am sure his daughter was tired of being cooped up with this strange, African tribe.

On June 3, 1947, I went into labor. I was early with this one, but we had just moved into a new, second-floor apartment in Altona and that may have had something to do with it. Fortunately, the hospital was just around the corner, so I could walk there while John watched the two children. It was spring, but as I observed on my way to deliver a third child by myself it was still extremely cold and muddy.

A pleasant, young nurse took me into my room and began to prep me, as my water had broken and I was in labor. I discussed with her the procedure as I had arranged it with my doctor. It was then that she informed me that my doctor was away in Winnipeg and, due to the late snow, it was unlikely he would get back in time. At that moment, a very young-looking man appeared and the nurse introduced him as an intern who would be assisting in the birth. She would be there, too, she comforted me – for she must have seen me pale at the thought of such a young man handling any delivery, let alone *my* delivery.

He washed his hands and put on a gown, then walked around to my knees and put my legs in stirrups. He looked up and informed me that I was dilated some and he would return in an hour to check me again. I was alone, cold and, as it turned out, quite properly worried.

He and the kind nurse returned sometime later. He checked me to discover that I was no further along and muttered to the nurse that he would have to "speed things up." The nurse demanded that he wait, but he did not. My arms were strapped to the bed, or else I would have escaped the room and his cruel work. Mercifully, they put me under ether for anesthesia and I was unconscious until little Lois was born.

I do not remember the moment of birth, only that the nurse put this blue, wet child in my shaking arms that were so terribly tired from fighting the straps so long. The doctor muttered to the nurse to clean me up as he stormed out, exhausted and sweating. She promised to report him for his abuse and unprofessional behavior. It didn't matter. I was alive and my baby was okay. Little Lois weighed just five pounds, but she had lots of hair and a cherubic, round face. I was too tired to cry with the joy I felt.

I knew I had torn badly, but the nurse was unwilling to suture me up herself. I adamantly refused to let that intern touch me again. John and the two children came later that day, and brought me flowers and drawings by the children to cheer me up. After a week of rest and holding my new baby, I was strong enough to walk home. I had no milk for this child, either. The weather had warmed some, but the mud was deep and slippery. It was a relief to be home and to share this tiny life with the other two children.

The bishop's daughter still came to babysit, and John and I took up deputation together again. The summer was drawing to a close and the mosquitoes swarmed in hordes. John's parents and siblings had little time for visiting, as their entire family – including small children – had to weed in the beet fields that stretched from one horizon to the next. They were paid cash for each row they weeded and none for those they didn't finish. This hard labor was their only income, thus they weeded in the rain, the cold, and in the heat and mosquitoes. John sometimes tried to help, but it was impossibly hard work even for him. Their state of extreme poverty unsettled me considerably. I did not know how to relate to them. I prayed for them and for guidance in being with them, but I never felt like part of the family.

We had traveled many miles and raised quite a bit of money. A kind family, the Penners, two brothers who ran a Dodge dealership in town, lent us a car – a model A Ford – for deputation. They loved to hear about Africa and gave generously to our fund. John was quite popular, but he held certain views theologically that went against the grain of Mennonite beliefs. He did not openly advocate his views, but word got around.

Late that summer, the church elders were called by the bishop to a meeting – a sort of trial, it turned out – to expose John's beliefs. John was asked to explain his views on several topics, but the ones they were waiting for were those on pacifism and eternal security. When he allowed that his beliefs differed with their teachings, they asked him to leave the church and revoked his status as a minister. That was bad enough because that meant the end of speaking and raising money in Mennonite churches. But then, the bishop refused to give us any of the money we had already raised.

We were devastated – and virtually broke. Had it not been for the kindness of the Penner brothers to give us cash under the table, we would have been in dire straits. I was beside myself with worry and three tiny children to tend in a small apartment. As if God knew my plight, we received a brochure advertising a mission conference in Montrose, Pennsylvania, to be held in September that very year. John wanted to go for refreshment, and so did I. I just wanted to get out of Canada for any reason right then!

We took every speaking engagement we could and saved our money to travel and pay for the Montrose conference. Lois was just three months old and although she was not gaining weight, she was healthy and so were the rest of us. It was a long trip, but we wanted to go. It had occurred to me that with three children, I wouldn't get to a single meeting, but we would at least be gone from this wasteland.

John asked his sister (who was married to the very bishop that had defrocked John) if Joanne could stay with her and her three daughters – all about the same age. She agreed, to my surprise and pleasure. We were down to two, but we had to get on the road if we were to make it, so off we four went. The Model A performed flawlessly. John was a superb mechanic. We decided to break the trip in Wheaton, Illinois, to see my younger sister Elsie, whose husband was studying at Wheaton College.

Elsie took one look at us and gasped. We silly people with that tiny baby were going "where?" she demanded to know. Then, she insisted that I leave Lois in her care till we came back. It was clearly what was best for Lois. That left us with Daniel only, and he learned quickly to sit quietly between us through the meetings so I could attend, too. It was a good week of spiritual and physical refreshment. We headed home with much needed joy and strength, picked up the two children and landed in our apartment to unwelcome cold. I never did grow accustomed to that cold!

The dreary cold and alienation of the place soon drove us to make plans to return to Lancaster. We could not endure another winter in Manitoba. We were both sure of that! So it was that on December 31, 1947, we boarded a train for Lancaster via New York and Niagara Falls—a sight we wanted the children to see.

Just about the time we crossed into the United States, however, little Lois broke out in a high fever. There was little we could do on the train. I swabbed her and gave her aspirin, but she was very sick when we got off the train in Lancaster a few days later.

We rushed her to the hospital to be told she had pneumonia. But, her lungs were clear. I knew that as a nurse, so I doubted that it was a pulmonary problem. They did give her antibiotics and she got better, so I was confused. We had moved into a new upstairs apartment, furnished this time by the church as a residence for furloughing missionaries. It was warm and well appointed, but it was upstairs – again. And I was, to be sure, pregnant – again.

Lois continued to come down with a strange fever that spiked very high at times. We would take her to the hospital, but no one could discover what caused it. We were busy by day with children and by night with speaking, so we had a variety of babysitters, young girls from the church to help us. One day, after we had come home and paid the girl, she left the apartment but failed to shut the door completely. It swung open and Lois, in her walker, tried to follow her and tumbled down that long flight of stairs. She lay silently quivering on the landing by the door.

I screamed and flew down the stairs to pick her up and hold her. She was limp. John heard my cry and rushed in to pick us both up, and we dashed to the hospital one more time. Lois had a mild concussion. However, in the course of multiple x-rays, they discovered that she had a congenitally deformed kidney. This was no doubt the cause of her fevers, for it created the conditions for frequent bladder and then kidney infections. She would later have surgery to remove the faulty organ and end her constant battle with infections and fever. God turned a near tragedy into triumph!

We had been on furlough for almost four years and the time for our

John's Dad was a skilled carpenter and here he begins to build the cab and box that would become a fine RV for safaris and medical clinics.

departure grew near. We were encouraged and so excited when the Penner brothers (our Dodge boys in Canada) told John they would provide him with a two-ton Dodge Power Wagon to take back to Africa. They donated the motor and frame, the rest was up to John.

John took the train to Altona and the Penner dealership in Canada. There, he saw his truck – four wheels on a frame with a motor – the highest thing on it the knob on the gear shift. He and his carpenter father then set about constructing a plywood and tin shell for the cab. John lashed a chair to the frame behind the steering wheel, pulled on some gloves, and drove the cab and frame back to Pennsylvania.

There, with the help of friends from church, he constructed a safari truck to end all safari trucks. It had airplane instruments and seats, a huge water tank under the back seat and a double bed folded up against one wall. It took him a full year to finish construction, load it with our goods like a container, and get it to the docks and on a freighter

For Mombasa. On the side of it, he had painted in Kikamba, "*Ngai ni wendo.*" God is love. We hoped to fly out in time to meet it in the port of Mombasa.

At about the time John was painting his precious truck a tan color to match the African dust, I went into labor with my fourth and last child. He drove me proudly to the hospital in it. I was very confident this time that I would receive proper, professional care. My doctor had already arranged

John and Alice proudly stand by their new safari vehicle at its dedication in Lancaster, cica 1950. The Kamba verse below the mission logo means: "God is love."

for a Caesarian delivery, since scarring had made it impossible for a normal delivery. He contended that I should have had a C-section for all of the others, too. No doubt!

John Stephen Schellenberg was born in the late morning of March 1, 1949. He weighed just over five pounds, and was healthy by the looks of him and his shock of red hair. I stayed in the maternity ward for a full week, giving him a bottle as I had no breast milk to offer him, either. After another week of rest, my dear doctor, Christian Wenger, did major reconstructive surgery on my lower anatomy, then I spent another week in recovery. I was able to keep the baby with me all of the time.

To say I was weak when I got out of the hospital would be an understatement. I was a frail mother of four – and pretty much alone – living in an upstairs apartment. I could barely manage getting all the kids fed and clothed. At night sleep was rare as all four seemed to cry at once. John snored through it all, tired as he was. I felt like a failure and found myself often alone and crying.

In my state, a dear friend from my past, Alice Rohrer, took me aside one day after church. She knew exactly what I was experiencing, and she said that she had made arrangements for me and John to go on a retreat to Ventnor, on the Jersey Shore, for a month. Joanne and Daniel would go to the Mennonite orphanage, and I could manage with Lois, now two, and Stephen, a month old. This I thought I could do.

We relaxed and enjoyed the time at the beach. But, when we returned, we found that Daniel had been cut severely on his leg while falling out of a metal wagon, and both older children seemed traumatized by their experiences. I felt exhausted most of the time. Then, a kind, young couple offered to help by taking Lois for a month. I needed the relief, and she gained some needed weight in their care.

We had somehow managed to raise not just our support for the next five years, but a good bit of money for travel and retirement. Calvary Church took on John's support full-time and that made the difference. Our income going back to Kenya the second time ranged from about $300 a month to as much as $400. With this, we paid for all our work expenses, travel and eventually, school fees for the older two.

Through it all, however, we learned that God provided and watched over us. We never lacked for our needs. When we had an unusual medical expense, a special gift would come just in time. I have to say that watching God provide money for us was a monthly miracle – a constant reminder of His care.

Life in America on that first furlough had been surprisingly hard. I was honestly looking forward to getting back to "normal" life in Kenya. We were thankful that the Field Council had seen fit to reassign us to Mbooni. No more mosquitoes, malaria and mambas! They had recognized our health problems and felt our family would be healthier at a higher altitude.

John and I were excited then on December 5, 1950, when the Dodge truck was on the high seas and all six of us were booked to fly out of New York for a stopover in South Hampton and then on to Nairobi, Kenya. A friend from the church with his truck delivered us to the New York airport.

Our flight was smooth and the kids were excited. Stephen actually slept most of the way across the Atlantic, and so did I. They must have known Mom and Dad were finally relaxed and free from constant missionary performance.

To my consternation, Britsh Overseas Airways Corporation had booked us on a seaplane for the last leg of our journey. It had pontoons! It looked so tiny rocking there by the pier. The pilot was no help either, as he tossed off the remark that it was his African "puddle jumper." But, we got in it anyway and buckled up tight. It roared out of the ocean spray, shaking mightily then quieted down as it lifted us into the blue sky of central Africa.

The small plane could not make enough altitude to need a pressurized cabin, so we were in what amounted to a tin can with loud engines throbbing next to us. The only compensation was that we had an amazing view of the African landscape sliding silently beneath our silver wings – its shadow tracing our route south. I was asleep for most of the first landings and refueling, and only awoke with the crashing thump as we hit the water and watched the spray blur the window view whenever we landed.

Finally, we were over the Great Rift Valley, and I knew we were close to Kenya and home. I woke the children to show them the snows of Mt. Kenya and the beautiful flamingo-covered, pink-tinted Lake Nakuru. We began our descent into the smaller Lake Naivasha in the shadow of the great volcanic rim of Mt. Longonot. I could not look out the window. I suddenly felt panicked – short of breath. I couldn't stop it. I moved to a seat next to John so I could hold his arm and weep. I know now that I was having a nightmare regression back to the sinking of the *Zamzam*, but all I could think of then was that we were all about to drown. I just couldn't shake the feeling.

I know I wanted to scream when we hit the water – bang! It sounded so much like the shell exploding next to my cabin. John patiently held me – the children secure in their seatbelts. Then, we slowed down with a swish, the engines throttled back and we bounced along the waves. We had landed safely. We were still in the palm of His hand!

I lifted my head in a moment, thanked God for letting me and my family land safely, and watched the yellow-fever trees on the shore of Lake Naivasha grow into their full stature. The beautiful waterbuck grazing beneath the yellow thorn trees did not even look up as the plane taxied into its berth.

The engines shut down and we were lashed up to the dock. The door opened and a grinning Sheldon Folk reached for the first of four children. John helped me out onto the wooden dock under the wing. I caught my balance on the floating pier, stood up and then felt the warm, African sun.

We were home at last!

A formal letter and a family portrait were all required to raise funds and inform prayer warriors who the Schellenberg family was that they supported. This was the formal portrait used in deputation for the Schellenberg family in 1950.

CHAPTER 8
Double-Edged Darkness

It was a tremendous relief to be assigned to a lush, green Mbooni station with the whole family. There was rain and food and even a grass lawn for the children to romp on. There were trees to climb and lovely flower gardens, too. The Power Wagon arrived safely with all our new equipment and we quickly set up housekeeping in the old, German, mud-walled house once again. We were unpacked and back to a normal routine in time for Christmas.

John had one of our workers climb a tall juniper tree in the yard and lop off the top for a Christmas tree. The smell of that fir by the fire and the sound of happy children waiting for Santa remains a strong memory in my mind at Christmas even today. John retired to his Santa workshop to build wooden toys – a tractor and barns for the boys and doll cradles for the girls. He teased the children with his stories of Mr. Goonerfitz, the legendary German elf, whom he said was secretly building Christmas toys whenever the children pestered him about what he was doing.

I was not assigned to the clinic this time since a young missionary, Carol Turner, lived next door to us and managed the dispensary. I was assigned to assist my husband in the pastor's school at Mbooni. John had felt that the

The children played in the dirt in front of the Bible school building with dorms upstairs and classrooms down. John's workshop and garage were housed in this large burnt brick building that John designed and built.

churches were growing in Ukambani, but they lacked strong, biblically – grounded pastors. John set about erecting a two-story brick school building with classrooms underneath and living quarters for the men above. He dug mud from the banks above the tennis court, then spread out thousands of bricks to dry on it before burning them for his building. It was clearly the proper use of a tennis court in Africa!

I had a concern for the pastors' wives, who had the responsibility for their large families as well as maintaining their role as "pastors' wives." The women needed guidance on the Christian family, nutrition, wifely duties to their husbands and, of course, how to entertain.

At that time, there were no materials printed for use in Bible or pastor's schools related to women, Christian ethics or practical living. My assignment was to write the most basic materials and teach them. What worked for me would then be revised and published for wider distribution. This assignment was an exciting challenge. I could set my own timetable and stay at home more. The children were older and largely entertained themselves, but I soon found that we as a family had many more visitors than ever before. Entertaining guests became a large part of my weekly responsibilities as well as expense. I have to say I enjoyed receiving guests, whether for a night or just for tea.

We settled in easily to life on Mbooni hill. We mostly attended church in the dark, wooden sanctuary near the primary school at the bottom of the hill. John mounted a large bell on the stump of a massive eucalyptus tree he had felled near the clinic, and it peeled out a call to worship every Sunday morning. Sometimes, we took a picnic and visited a remote, young church fellowship. That Dodge Power Wagon made overnight stays very easy, no matter how remote the location.

One of the most important activities in which our entire family engaged was the spreading of printed tracts with stories and the way of salvation in them. John translated a story like the little hen who gave her life in a fire by covering her chicks to save them. Jesus was equated with the mother hen, giving his life for mankind. This story then was printed on colored paper which all of us sat around the table to fold. John had a special box in the big truck just behind his head where he stuffed as many colored tracts as he could before a trip. As we passed people walking along the road, the children enjoyed holding out the colored leaflets and letting them go to watch them flutter in the dust and fall at the native's feet. Over the years we passed out hundreds of pounds of these gospel tracts as we drove along in our truck. The children, especially, enjoyed this part of sharing the gospel.

A year flew by, then John and I had to confront perhaps the most difficult disruption of our family life and relaxed lifestyle. It was September, 1951, and

One of the most painful decisions for any missionary parent was to send seven year olds off to boarding school for the first time. Here is Joanne at seven dressed in her braids and RVA uniform—a brave little girl!

our oldest daughter, Joanne, was now seven years old. It was time to send her off to boarding school.

The problem was that the largest tribe in Kenya, the Kikuyu, were expressing growing discontent with the colonial rule of the British, which included the loss of much of their tribal land to the Crown. A family of white settlers had been slaughtered by rebels on the Kinangop, just a few miles from Kijabe station and the Rift Valley Academy boarding school for missionary children – our Joanne. This was among the first attacks in what the British would call the Mau Mau Emergency.

The question of refusing to send Joanne to boarding school never arose in our minds. Home-schooling was unheard of at that time. We simply packed her trunk with clothes and shoes for a three-month "term," or semester, and dropped her off in the care of missionaries we hardly knew. She would be home for Christmas, and we prayed for her mightily while she was at RVA as a tiny child.

It was cold there and the food for nearly one hundred students that year was prepared by a British settler's wife, who kindly offered to cook. Her understanding of child nutrition, however, seemed highly suspect. She could serve macaroni and cheese, corn bread and a white cake with icing all at one meal. Ketchup was apparently a vegetable. She regularly sent children who laughed or talked too loudly to the principal for discipline. Hers was a no-nonsense dining hall! The children wore uniforms that included a light sweater during rainy seasons, which could drop temperatures at that altitude to almost freezing. Life had to be very regimented for everyone – staff included.

By the first holiday, Joanne was bursting with excitement to come home. She wrote us letters every week. She had made straight A's in first grade. We were relieved that not a single Mau Mau incident had threatened her safety – or ours. She went back to RVA to finish the spring term, then came home for a month of holiday and fattening up on good cooking.

While Joanne was away at school, we had employed a new *aya* (babysitter) named Ruthie, whom the three younger children just loved. She would load them up with firewood or go in the garden and pick fruit and vegetables. She played endlessly with them, and it was her patience and creativity that allowed me to do what my heart called me to do—teach African women the principles of a Christian home.

From my experience in nursing during my first term, I had observed that many young Christian mothers had no understanding of the difference between a pagan way of raising children and a Christian way. I began by helping them understand that a Christian family has a certain structure of authority that God has ordained. The husband, even if he is not a practicing Christian, was still God's chosen vessel for authority, which a good wife must obey. If a wife obeys her husband, then she can expect her children to obey her and respect both parents.

Under the authority of the husband, a Christian woman had certain duties different from him. She was primarily responsible for keeping the house neat and tidy and preparing nutritious food. She would raise the children. I had seen many mothers begin to wean their children from breast milk and stuff solid maize and beans into the baby's mouth. Of course, many of the children would be almost two when weaning commenced, since nursing was a traditional method of birth control – or, I should say, spacing. Nonetheless, transition to solid food was important and too often not well managed.

When bottled soda water, especially Fanta Orange, became available in every shop in every village, mothers often thought that they were giving their children orange juice and that drinking this would make their babies healthy and modern. What feeding Fanta did was make their babies fat and listless, then put them into catastrophic decline until they had to go to some hospital with acute malnutrition. Hospitals in Nairobi had entire wards for "Fanta babies" on the verge of death. Understanding and coping with modernity was a major challenge for rural people emerging from paganism.

Money was not a subject to be taught to women back in the 1950s. Today, development projects lend money to women, but not then. Women did sell some food and baskets and could earn a little money. The smallest coins all had holes in them, and women would slip them onto a leather thong they tied around their waists. It was a not a good idea for a woman to display too many coins if she didn't want them converted to snuff or local beer by her husband or brother. Accounting was best left to men in 1950! We encouraged the women to hide their cash.

Perhaps the most important, and certainly the most appreciated, class that I taught was a class on etiquette. I taught the men first, then at the end of a term, their wives. Many leaders were increasingly required to meet and sometimes dine with colonial officers. Kamba men wanted to know how to engage in polite conversation, then how to eat in front of whites so that neither they nor their hosts would be uncomfortable.

I taught them how to set a table, and which fork or spoon to use and in which order. They learned how to initiate a conversation and politely get food passed. For example, one never should ask for the salt and pepper directly. One does not say, "Please pass me the salt." One should rather say, "Would you care for some salt?" Such delicate diplomacy as to how one passes the salt has been lost on all but the most dignified today—even in England, where such manners came from! It might sound silly now, but I received more letters of thanks for this course than any other. My book on these matters, however, never did get published. Neither did my books on children's health and nutrition.

John and I enjoyed our work at Mbooni. We got to go on safari and even took a vacation to the coast at Christmas 1951. No more malaria, and only once did the children see a cobra snake in the cluster of bamboo at the bottom of the yard. But, I didn't have to pass there daily anymore! Sadly, our peaceful little bit of paradise was about to be disrupted.

On October 20, 1952, the colonial government declared a State of Emergency in Kenya. In the Central Province of Kenya, which surrounded Nairobi, certain elements of the largest tribe, the Kikuyu, were rising up to protest the loss of their land to the British. They wanted independence from Britain and they demanded that all white settlers leave their tribal lands. The British called this largely Kikuyu uprising the Mau Mau Emergency, which officially lasted until 1955.

The Kikuyu protest was led by a British-educated intellectual, Jomo Kenyatta, who, incidentally, had an English wife. Kenyatta ran the political arm of the protest, but then the Kikuyu also began a violent wing called the Kenya Land and Freedom Army, under General China. To this day, missionaries disagree as to the purpose of this rebellion and the need for the extreme measures with which Britain chose to repress it. Ironically, fewer whites were killed by rebels than died in automobile accidents during the entire time of the revolt. On the other hand, thousands of Africans died on both sides of the struggle. I say "both sides" because there were two sides, and we felt that the "right" side was defending the British order and authority. Many African Christians refused to take an oath to destroy colonial rule and they suffered for this. We came to feel that there was a Satanic force behind the Mau Mau rebellion with its beastly oathings.

In response to Kikuyu violence, the British rounded up whole villages and placed them in security settlements. Anyone found outside the surrounding stockades at night was automatically deemed a terrorist and summarily executed or detained – often tortured. John witnessed some of this treatment and was horrified that an Englishman could brutalize another human being so.

For our part, we taught our pastors that this revolt was unethical and against the Biblical teaching that it was God who ordained all authority on the earth. We discouraged our people on Mbooni hill from submitting to forced oathing, which the Mau Mau required to assure loyalty to their cause. We came to believe that the strength of our churches reduced the threat of Mau Mau on our hill.

However, one evening in October that year, the British District Officer came to warn us of rumors that a "gang" of Mau Mau were hiding in the area to "terrorize" whites and recruit Kamba to their cause. He suggested we get a gun and have a plan for what to do in case of an attack. Oddly, he refused to lend John a gun. He also refused to post an armed guard on the station with its two single white women.

What we decided to do was to prepare a safe room in the attic of the old house. We could open the drawers in the bathroom, climb up through a hatch to a platform on the ceiling timbers and close the hatch. The kids would climb up there while John and I would fight off anyone who got in the house using our machetes – called *pangas* in Kenya. The children had bottles and rocks to throw on any attackers. Brave as this plan of ours was, it was perfectly foolish and doomed to fail.

We only had one occasion to rush the children up to their safe loft when we thought we heard Mau Mau drive up in a truck and charge onto our front veranda. Our best defense, it turned out, was silence and intense prayer. Whoever it was, they never smashed the glass front door and came in. I reflect on this moment now and I realize that I had no idea where we kept the *pangas* – nor could I have used one. God was our refuge, our fortress in time of trouble. If God be for us, then who can be against us?

In the early 1950s, the word "Kenya" was synonymous with the Mau Mau. That movement captured the minds and the headlines of the world when anyone thought about Africa. But, to tell the truth, across Ukambani in general and on Mbooni hill in particular, the movement had little impact on ordinary, daily life.

A far more intense battle raged for the hearts and minds of the people in the villages and forests of Mbooni hill—witchcraft! Kenya faced double-edged darkness! Witchcraft seemed to hover over the land like a wraith, unseen but felt. The forces of darkness and Satan were so powerful that they controlled how people dressed, planted their food and even named their children. I came to call the whole lot of it "paganism." It was against this culture of darkness that John and I felt we did battle.

On Mbooni hill, there was no witch more powerful for many years than one known as Syo Mbole. People feared her so much that when she approached, they would not even look at her. She arrayed herself in black clothes, and magic talismans hung from her body and clothes. Her ankles had bracelets that announced her coming with a strange, jangling sound that sent a chill up even my spine.

She was darkness and evil incarnate. But, she was also a vulnerable human being, and I came to see her as "possessed" and desirous of freedom. She would come to the clinic before she became so powerful, and sit and listen to the Gospel story that some pastor or one of the dressers would share before we opened for treatment. She would mock the pastors and belittle them for their fear, but she did come for "white" medicine. And, she and her children did get well.

I knew that she knew we had more powerful medicine and a more powerful God and spirit within us than she did. We prayed for her and a number of other witches under her tutelage. The drums reminded us every night how long it would take to change this culture.

I cannot tell you the joy I felt when she came to church one day in a new dress, wearing a colorful headscarf and shoes! She wanted to be saved and join the church. She was eventually baptized in the river, then set a date to burn all of her witchcraft paraphernalia on the church grounds.

What an amazing display of power that fire and that triumphant singing made as she and others burned their bows and arrows, poisons, even their old clothes. She wanted to be absolutely free of all paganism. Ordinary Christians in the church could hardly believe that this fearsome woman was one of them, now humble, quiet and full of child-like faith.

She became a dear friend of mine in those last years of our second term. She was older then I, with her own family and gardens. I went to visit her one day, and I asked her just exactly how she came to be saved and to be released from demonic powers. Her answer surprised me.

She told me that many years ago when I was working in the clinic, she would come to watch me. She thought I was maybe a "white witch," and needed to learn my powers and potions since I appeared to be her most serious competition. In the course of sitting on the grass alone at the clinic, a dresser had given her a small book. He called it the *Wordless Book*. It had a green cover with several colored pages, which were code for the way of salvation, once someone explained what each color meant. There were no words in this booklet. We gave out thousands of them as they were self-teaching, and the Gospel could easily be passed by word of mouth to many others.

She told me that she had hidden the tiny book in her hut walls and would take it out to "read" it when she felt powerless. She said that it made a great deal of sense to her. The green pages told her that once the world was perfect and beautiful. That agreed with the Kamba myth of creation, she told me. She knew that the first page was probably true. The next page was black. She knew personally that Satan and sin were real and had come to darken the world – her world! The next page was red and she knew, too, that without the shedding of blood, there was no remission of sin. Even the Kamba believed that. A sacrifice had to be made so that a substitute could take her place and she did not have to die. That sacrificial lamb was Jesus, she had learned. She believed that and received Jesus into her heart all alone in her hut. She was forgiven for all her sin. The next page was white and it told her that all her sins were gone – forgiven. The power of evil and darkness were defeated. She would live in the light now.

The last page of the precious book was gold. What she said next was the sur-

A classic Kamba village of grass-thatched mud huts in baobab, circa 1950. The young woman in the foreground is weaving a sisal basket as she walks home carrying water on her back in a calabash gourd.

prise. She told me that she had begun this whole move toward the light and Jesus because of the last page – the gold one. She did not want to come back as another human being or an animal to this earth and its misery and death, as her traditional religion taught her. The promise of heaven and light and beauty drew her, irresistibly, to the Gospel. She wanted eternal life with God in heaven. There would be water and food and no tears.

So many missionaries questioned that little book, but they forgot that God has chosen the foolish things of this world to confound the wise. You sow the seed however and wherever you can, and reap a great harvest! No missionary could have ever been as effective in bringing women to Christ and freedom from the demonic as Syo Mbole.

By the second year of the Mau Mau rebellion, it was Daniel's turn to go to boarding school, as he was almost eight years old in September of 1952. Joanne could help her little brother make the transition. It was fun getting the uniforms and shoes made in Machakos town. The two of them looked so cute and so fragile in their uniforms with their skinny legs sticking out. My heart would have broken, but what good would it do to cry? No use upsetting them, I told myself.

The day came to put their trunks in the big Power Wagon (with "God is love" painted on the side) and head some one hundred miles through Nairobi and up over the escarpment of the Great Rift Valley to boarding school. The long rains had just broken, and John knew that the river at the bottom of Mbooni hill would be deep and dangerous. Rose Horton decided to ride down to Machakos with us, so I got in the back with four children and we slithered down the hill to the first river.

We got to the river and, as predicted, it was swollen, muddy and angry. Six inches of moving floodwater could carry a car. This was three or four feet of deep, raging water. John got out and made a mark on the upper, visible bit of concrete above the water line. We waited an hour to see if the river was rising or falling. It was rising and it was time to go, if we were ever going to go. The kids would miss supper if we arrived late.

John double-clutched the big truck into low gear to save his battery and crept into the water, which rushed up in a huge back wave against the wheels and then the door. He inched deeper into the river until the waves were almost at his window, then gunned the engine to make a bow wave so as to reduce the load of water against the vehicle and maybe get through the worst part. We had our eyes closed. For this move to fail was certain death, and all that was visible anyway was swirling, dirty water – our grave. I yelled at John to pray, and he yelled back that that was what he was doing!

The engine choked and coughed and the truck jerked to a halt. The engine died. Rose began to scream. I prayed out loud while John stomped the starter. It wouldn't crank. All four children were frozen stiff – we were going to die.

John then grabbed the carpet on the floor, climbed out the window, over the hood and onto the front fender. He opened the hood, dried the spark-plug cap with his handkerchief, then placed the mat over the engine and got back in the cab. He ground the truck into first gear again and pumped the starter, which jerked the car forward a foot with each push. After what seemed like an eternity, we slowly emerged from the torrent. We were soaked, and way too scared to say anything or move. Rose was chalk white and paralyzed in the front seat.

Suddenly we heard a cheer—*"Wazungu, wazungu!"* While we were concentrating so hard, a bus full of Africans headed up the hill had pulled up to the crossing. We had provided hilarious entertainment for them, it seemed. Their term for all whites was *"Wazungu"* – the people who run around in circles till they get dizzy! We were pretty dizzy that day.

After that "crossing of the Red Sea," the rest of the trip was uneventful, notwithstanding the fact that we drove for fifty miles through a deep forest in Mau Mau country with no armed escort and along such muddy roads that many other families were stuck. Not John in his Power Wagon!

As we drove up to the main dormitory, called Kiambogo (whose corner stone had been laid by Teddy Roosevelt in 1907), we were shocked. Had we not been late, perhaps we would have turned around. The school was surrounded by tall, concertina, razor-wire fences. Inside them were deep ditches filled with sharpened bamboo staves—*punji* sticks, they were called in Vietnam. Huge floodlights were already on and they illuminated four massive sandbag forts bristling with 50-caliber machine guns.

The meaning of Mau Mau finally struck us. The school was in a war zone. Worst of all, a contingent of African soldiers was bivouacked just below the main girls dormitory. Their British commanding officer, Mr. Chips, quartered himself in the senior boys dormitory. I can hardly think back to that moment even today. My only hope and prayer was that God would wrap my two tiny children tightly and protect them from what I would not let my mind imagine.

We deposited the children as the last bell for supper rang. We kissed the two terrified oldest children goodbye, then I went up and made their beds and unpacked their clothes. I had bought each a small toy to make the loss they would feel that night a little more bearable. I placed these toys under their pillows. I just steeled myself to not express what I was feeling. We drove back to Mbooni that night through the mud and a river that was, thankfully, far lower than in the morning. Poor Rose refused to ride home with us.

Life was not the same during the five years of Kenya's Mau Mau rebellion. Lancaster bombers flew sorties over the Great Rift Valley, where the children could watch their bombing raids. When terrorists were suspected of approaching the school, the bells rang and students of all sizes had to pull their mattresses onto the floor and hide below the windows. One night, a massive attack occurred on the hill above the school when a gang of Mau Mau burned down a village called Larri, killing hundreds of loyalist Kikuyu.

It was rumored that this gang actually intended to kill the children of missionaries because that would frighten the whites into leaving Kenya. If they actually attacked, I don't know, but it was rumored that they did and that a huge, white wall appeared around the school and stopped them. Detainees in a concentration camp who became Christians told of this miracle to save RVA. I took great comfort from that story!

Fortunately, nothing happened to us or to our two children in boarding school throughout the years of Mau Mau. In 1955, the emergency was over and a relative calm returned to the country.

Not long after that, John and I packed up our household things and put them in storage. We were due another furlough and our whole family would soon return to America. Joanne was now in junior high and an accomplished pianist. She would play the pump organ and her father played his violin on many an evening around the fire at Mbooni.

We hadn't had a family holiday for many years, with funds short and Mau Mau interfering with travel, so we decided to take a ship from Europe to New York on our way home. That floating holiday was a highlight of our tour for everyone in our family. The luxury liner we boarded was none other than the *Queen Mary*. We all felt like royalty. We ate heartily and often – once even at the Captain's table. Who knows when perfect manners may be needed?

CHAPTER 9
A Royal Tea Party

Calvary Independent Church kindly prepared a three-bedroom apartment for our family when we got back to America in the spring of 1956. It was, unfortunately, an upstairs apartment – again. This time, I was not pregnant! We were so shocked to find it full of clothing and everything we could possibly need for our year of furlough. The generosity and kindness of church folk and even neighbors were overwhelming. My dad gave us his used car, since he was no longer secure as a driver given his age. It was a 1949 Pontiac sedan, but it hauled our family around just fine. John was such a good mechanic that it never let us down on the road.

The children were enrolled directly into good, neighborhood schools. It was such a relief that they could walk safely to school with other kids. They got involved in after-school events and sports, and enjoyed the social life for children that the church offered. We were well received and we found deputation a good deal easier than the first time.

We settled into a routine family life and when school was out for the summer, we decided to take a trip to visit the family in Canada. John bought a large, canvas, ex-military tent that must have weighed a ton. We tied the luggage on the top of the old Pontiac, stuffed the tent into the trunk and took off for Canada. John decided the tires would not make it if he drove over 50 miles per hour, so journey was mind-numbingly slow. No amount of games could make eight hours of droning, dreary travel pass quickly enough even for compliant kids like ours. We stopped for picnics since fast food was not yet common and restaurants were far too costly for our budget.

Every evening as it got dark, John would pull off the main highway and start down some rural lane. He would spot a farmhouse and drive up to it, get out and explain our situation to the owners. He politely asked if we could pitch a tent somewhere and spend the night on their property. It was embarrassing for me and must have been beyond humiliating to the children. We should never have been embarrassed. Not a single time on that trip to and from Canada did a single family ever turn us down or think it weird.

In fact, they often invited us in for food and gave us eggs and milk. I sometimes felt like they must have just been waiting for us to show up. Maybe they were and God had brought us together. Our routine must have been comical to watch. We would struggle to get the tent up, make some food on the camp stove, spread out the sleeping bags, have devotions and try to get some sleep. After the kids were down, John and I would often go to the house of our hosts and witness or share stories of Africa. I think we learned something about the big hearts and generosity of Americans we would never have known without those awkward intrusions into strangers' lives.

We drove through hundreds of miles of amber waves of grain and spotted more tornadoes than we wanted to, then crossed the Canadian border and on to Altona, Manitoba, again. This time, it was wet but not so cold. A great deal of the poverty of a few years ago was not so visible. We stayed in a huge farmhouse owned by John's sister, Elizabeth, whose husband was the bishop who presided over our tribulation the last time. He was retired now and a very wealthy man from farming flax. None of the animosity and intrigue from before lingered, and John's extended family seemed happier than ever. Our children got along well with their peers. We were so pleased to see this.

To our surprise and extreme pleasure, the Penners (our Canadian Dodge boys) donated a brand-new Dodge pickup truck for our use on our next term in Kenya. John built a camper top on it and bolted a seat in the back for three kids. We would drive home with more room and much less stress over whether this vehicle would make it.

We had to return to the United States to put the children back in school in Lancaster at the end of that summer. When their school year was up, it was time to pack again and head back to Kenya. We all passed our medical exams and were cleared to return by AIM in New York. Calvary Church continued our full support – to our great relief!

The children went right back to RVA as soon as we got off of the freighter, which we had traveled on to give us some added rest before jumping back into the work. Our truck was with us and so were our crates of household effects. We enjoyed stopping at all the ports along the eastern seaboard of Africa. The children especially enjoyed Lourenzo-Marques, (now Maputo, Mozambique, a former Portuguese colony) with its tree-lined boulevards, European shops, ice cream and, most of all, a fantastic zoo and aviary.

We were assigned to Machakos this term. John was to head the pastor's school there instead of at Mbooni station because so many complained that it was cold and too hard to get to. We went up to Mbooni and moved our stuff to Machakos. Our house was once again a very old, brown, German-built, mud-walled bungalow. It was very similar to the house at Mbooni, so it remained cool in the heat and warm in the cold, rainy season.

I was assigned to teach in the local Bible school just down the hill from our house. I also had to run the Ukambani bookstore. I kept the accounts, filled out orders and mailed hundreds of books a year. I was also responsible for printing and reprinting popular books. I did a great deal of walking up and down that hill, so when I say I "ran" the bookstore, I should say, rather, that it "ran" me.

I did enjoy my teaching, but it turned out to be more stressful than I had anticipated because I had to write a new curriculum every semester. There was just no material in print to teach women about nutrition, childcare and the Christian home – all dear to my heart. And, of course, there was always my favorite subject – etiquette!

About the third year into this assignment, John was elected by his fellow missionaries to be the chairman of the AIM Ukambani stations combined. This task included running meetings, lots of travel and a great deal of entertaining for me—and thus expense. It seemed like every day

I would have guests for one meal or another. I would run up the hill to check on the food and dining room settings, then rush back to class. I had a fantastic crew of cooks and a houseboy, but for some reason, I had to keep my finger on the pulse of the place. It was fun when it was happening, but then in the evenings, I would find myself quite weary and John would gently help me into bed.

I truly needed a vacation, but what I got instead was another assignment. I look back now and wonder why I accepted it, but back then, I didn't question either my strength or the possibility of saying no.

It so happened that every year, the entire missionary family of AIM in Kenya would gather for an annual conference. RVA boarding school was the only place big enough to house and feed everyone, so it always happened at Kijabe. And, it happened in December, just before Christmas when it was wet and cold. Each year, a different regional group was given the task of organizing this conference for other missionaries. It involved planning meals, scheduling special speakers and assigning every family a place to stay. It was a full-time job for anyone asked to do it.

It so happened that the year before I was asked, those who had put on the conference had done a very poor job by all accounts, and the formal evaluations that had come in confirmed it. I was asked to run the show because they wanted the food perfect and the entire experience to be seamless. It was a compliment and, at that time, I had no defense against what it would take to meet their extremely high expectations. I was already exhausted and overloaded. I wonder now what was I thinking.

But, being tired was not anything unusual and I set about for an entire year, mostly every evening, to make this next conference perfect. I had some help from near-by missionary friends on the station, but I was not so good at delegating. Somehow, I felt that all of this was on my shoulders alone.

The kids came home for vacation that year and were excited about Christmas and even the coming conference. They could make some cash from tips doing odd jobs, serving tables and washing dishes. I was dreading the event, going over list after list. We loaded up the truck and drove to Nairobi, where we packed it full of fresh fruit, vegetables and flowers from the huge market in the middle of town.

By the time we got out of Nairobi, it was late afternoon and I was in a panic – I did not want to be late to get dinner going for the huge crowd sure to descend upon the school that evening. I can remember driving up to the

Great Rift Valley escarpment with its hazy blue view of Suswa and Longonot craters directly in front of us, and Kijabe hill waiting to erupt on our right. The road snaked along the escarpment and we had to watch for fallen rocks. John pulled off at the first lookout to let us all see the magnificent view of the Great Rift Valley falling away below the steep precipice on which we stood.

Suddenly, I went into what I now know was a panic attack. The air was thin and I was stressed beyond my capacity to bear. Suddenly, I could not catch my breath. My hands turned blue and began to curl up. I cried – and I could not stop. The children went into shock. I could see what was going on around me, but I was powerless to speak or to stop this overwhelming sense of dread. I couldn't move and I think I must have passed out. I remember nothing until I awoke in the hospital late that night.

John wisely did not take me to Kijabe, even though there was a hospital there. Instead, he drove at some speed to Nairobi hospital, where I was sedated and made to rest. I was exhausted and dehydrated. I stayed for a few days in the hospital, then I went to recover my strength to a marvelous sanatorium called St. Julian's, near Limuru, just outside of Nairobi.

I spent a month there, eating good food, walking in their spectacular gardens and praying. Of course, I was ashamed and could hardly face the ladies I had betrayed or the mission leaders, who probably wondered if I had lost my mind. John and the children came to see me from the conference first, then once a week from Machakos. There was no talking during meals and no running allowed on the richly landscaped grounds, so the kids didn't like being there and they didn't stay long.

I did recover my strength and sorted out a number of issues in my life, which time at St. Julian's enabled me to think about. We had one year left in our term and it had to go well. The children were now older and Joanne would graduate from high school in one year. After that, we planned to stay home in America so we could support the older children in college. This, then, would be our last major effort in Ukambani for a while. I was able to finish writing all my desired curricula and put the bookstore on sound financial footing.

The one thing that began to dominate all conversation and much of the media that year, was the coming of independence to the colony of Kenya. The air was thick with fear for most of the white settlers. Many were selling off their land and moving to Rhodesia or South Africa. Jomo Kenyatta was released from prison and he would soon be elected Kenya's first president.

We did not know what "Uhuru" (Independence, in Kiswahili) would mean for the churches of AIM. There was talk of kicking out the missionaries and taking over the work. The problem with that, they soon realized, was that with the missionaries went their money. That wouldn't do!

As the time for the actual event of independence drew closer, we could feel the excitement and anticipation of a great moment in history of which we would be a part. To our surprise, and probably because John was still the Chairman of the Mission in Ukambani, we got invited to the festivities leading up to the big day. We were already booked to leave Kenya for furlough just before Independence Day, but we as a family could participate in the festivities before it.

The headline event we all wanted to see was the visit (on her birthday) of Princess Margaret. She was coming to Machakos as a part of her visit to Kenya. She was on her way to Tsavo Natural Park and agreed to spend an hour watching native dancing and greeting the Kamba. She could not have failed to know that the Kamba tribesmen made up nearly half of all of her loyal troops, the famous King's African Rifles. The British government paved the dirt road from the main Mombasa road to Machakos in record time. Ten miles of tarmac in ten days! Such speedy roadwork was unheard of.

The big day of her visit dawned bright and clear, to everyone's relief. We were in the VIP section, roped off from thousands of cheering and flag-waving school children and villagers. The gleaming Land Rover with a glass top entered the football stadium and drove slowly around the perimeter for all to see Her Royal Majesty. She wore a peach chiffon dress with an overcoat and a matching hat and gloves. She stood on a metal stand that allowed her to hold on to a bar as she waved through the glass. All that was visible were her shoulders and head as she passed by.

She stepped down from the Land Rover and walked through a reception line to her dias. Little girls handed her flowers and curtsied. Chiefs and government officials bowed and she curtsied back. It was all a very formal and proper affair.

What followed next was a display of traditional dancing that must remain as the high-water mark of gymnastic wonder. Over all the years that we had watched fantastic Kamba dancing, this display was unparalleled. The moves by those young men and women were so difficult and so dangerous as to take your breath away! The dust settled from the dancers, then a massive display of military troops and machinery marched by her dias in dress parade. We jumped in our car and drove out the newly paved road to wait for her to pass. I can still see our children lined up, waving their flags. She actually waved and smiled at us in return.

What a day it had been! But, the festivities were not over. I had one more big surprise. John had just received an invitation to have tea with Her Royal Majesty, Princess Margaret, in one week. I had brought a lovely, light-brown dress from America with matching accessories—all but the shoes I wanted for just such an affair. My hat and gloves and purse all matched. I only lacked proper high-heeled shoes.

For those, I drove into Nairobi, where the best shoemaker in Kenya, Mr. Pardiwalla, squatted in his shop on Biashara street. I was no stranger to him, but he never acted like he knew me. I'm sure he was only interested in how much he could make and, in the process, he clearly enjoyed the exchange of bargaining, which I happened to be good at and enjoyed. I showed him a picture from a Sears catalogue of the shoes I wanted him to make. I needed them in one week. This, he was certain, could not be done. Not for my price. He wanted more money. I offered more. He didn't accept, but told me to come back for his best price that afternoon. I left after he drew my foot on a piece of dirty brown paper.

When I showed up that same afternoon, he had the shoes already made and they fit perfectly. He knew he had me and could get his "best price." And, he did. No matter. I had my shoes! So I was, at last, totally ready for a royal tea party.

The big day came and I took my dress in the car with John to Nairobi. No children were allowed. This tea was to be held at the formal gardens of the British High Commission. It was by invitation only. We had our printed card and I hurriedly dressed at Mayfield. I would wear my flat-soled shoes until we were ready to get out of the car. Then, we drove to the gardens, where we saw a long line waiting to be introduced and to shake hands with Princess Margaret herself.

I got out of the car, pulled on my new high-heeled shoes, giddy with excitement, and promptly fell down. The heel of my right shoe had snapped off. What was I to do? There was no time to fix it. John came from parking the car and he tried to get it to stick on properly. We tried cactus juice, even some chewing gum. It was no use.

The line was moving and I in it, pretending that my heel was just fine. I chatted rather too excitedly to those around and stepped as carefully as I could. I practiced all the way up to the moment of truth. Would my years of training in etiquette carry me through this crisis with sufficient charm and grace?

I stepped up to Princess Margaret and curtsied. She offered me her hand. I shook it and almost fainted. She was so radiant and so gracious, I doubt seriously that if I had limped she would have cared. We moved on and I asked John to take me home. No tea for me that day. My leg muscles were cramping and I was exhausted from the stress, even if the experience was truly a moment of great triumph for me personally.

We flew out of Kenya just weeks before Independence Day. I have to say that the memory of that royal tea party and the joyful anticipation of so many Africans on the occasion of their independence remains very powerful to this day. Jomo Kenyatta wrote a book just before Uhuru, in which he promoted reconciliation between the colonialists and the colonized because they would soon be equals. He titled his book, *Suffering without Bitterness*. I wanted that to be true of me, too.

CHAPTER 10
Farewell to Africa

We flew out of Kenya in July of 1963. The country was on the threshold of Independence and a great deal of excitement filled the air. We had our own final bit of excitement ourselves as our oldest daughter, Joanne, had just graduated from RVA. And, to add to that joy, she had also won first place in the prestigious Kenya Music Festival's open piano competition. We were a proud and happy family flying off to Europe for a brief bit of tourist travel before settling down in America for an extended leave.

John and I had made up our minds that we would take a leave of absence from the mission field, to make a home for the children to ease their transition to life in America and to get them into college. But first, we knew that they were all old enough to enjoy some of the world's most important cultural sites in Europe. This trip would be their last opportunity to see important landmarks in world history.

We landed in Egypt first and stayed with our missionary friends, the Hoffmeiers, who had served in Egypt as long as we had in Kenya. Their fluency in Arabic made our excursion to the pyramids so much

The children enjoyed a camel ride in Cairo, Egypt, and stopped for a photo in front of the Sphinx with the great pyramid of Cheops and its alabaster-tiled point in the background.

richer. We left Egypt for Jordan and the amazing experience of walking in the Holy Land. Our guide was an Arab Christian, and he chauffeured us everywhere from King Davids' summer home in Dothan to the Dome of the Rock in Jerusalem. We drove down the rocky road to Jericho and on down to the Dead Sea, where the children all got to float in the salty water. We visited Bethlehem, Gethsemane, the Mount of Olives and so much more. All of it made the New Testament and the life of Christ very real for all of us.

We left the heat and crowded streets of the Middle East and landed in Rome next. We did get to see St. Peter's Basilica, but not much else because John fell quite sick the first night. No one wanted to risk getting around without him, and he could not get out of bed until we were forced to get on the train that would take us across Italy, through Switzerland and down to Rotterdam in The Netherlands. That train ride turned out to be a nightmare. We managed to get on the wrong train, or at least the wrong "class" compartment, and had to put up with wooden benches crowded with peasants and their produce, picnics and wine.

After our two oldest entered college at Millersville University, we bought this house nearby so they cold live at home and focus on studies.

We didn't see much of the countryside, needless to say. Fortunately, we had booked tickets on the *Queen Elizabeth II* liner for a week of rest and good food before we landed in New York.

John was much better by the time we got to Lancaster, and we found the church missionary home on Wabank Street once again completely outfitted for our family. Joanne went off to study music at Moody Bible Institute, and Daniel and the two younger ones went to local schools. John and I quickly realized that we would have four children leaving the nest in the next few years. Until then, they would need a place to stay and our support through college.

We therefore took our leave of absence from AIM Kenya and bought a house in Millersville, Pennsylvania. Yes, indeed, it was, once again, an upstairs apartment. We had to build two rooms in the attic for the boys and then we had enough bedrooms. As a Canadian, John could not earn much money, but he went to work next door at Millersville State College (now Millersville University) as a janitor at night to earn his limit. I renewed my nursing license and went on duty at Calvary Fellowship Homes. Joanne transferred to Millersville from Moody and Dan was accepted there as well. Lois and Steve walked across the street to Penn Manor High School.

We stayed in Millersville until the two oldest children had graduated from college and the girls were married. Steve was studying at LeTourneau College in Texas, and Dan was back in Kenya as a headmaster in a government school.

We sold the house in Millersville and answered a call from AIM Kenya to return to teach at the newly formed Scott Theological College at Machakos. We stayed there for two years – until 1970. The highlight of that time in Kenya for me was planning Dan's wedding in Limuru, Kenya, to his high-school sweetheart, Cathy Boone, whose parents were Southern Baptist medical missionaries in Uganda.

With our contract at Scott College complete, John and I had an opportunity to move to Okanagan Bible College in British Columbia, Canada, where John taught Bible and I was the Dean of Women for three years. John had always wanted to finish his Ph.D. in Theology, and he was accepted at Trinity College in Florida to do so. After he received his doctorate, he stayed on to teach, and I was asked to be the Dean of Women there, too.

In 1975, AIM Kenya begged us to come back to teach at Scott Theological College in Machakos for second time. We were not very retired anyway, so we said we would. Various people made up our support, but among them, Dr. And Mrs. Thoms of Houston, did the lion's share – and continued to do so for some time, even after we retired and after John died. We had a contract to teach at Scott for two years. Dan

First day of studies in America.

and Cathy and their four children were living just down the hill near Machakos town at that time. They were working with the Southern Baptists. We got to relate to the three grandchildren and baby-sat them while Cathy delivered her last baby in Nairobi. I could hardly keep up with the children.

All of my adult life, I had suffered from severe bunions and corns on both feet. The pain became severe, so I decided to have surgery at Kijabe to remove the pesky growths. I went to the hospital and John came up later to pick me up. During the night that he arrived, he began to cough. It was a cough so loud and so unusual that it caused the neighbors to wake up. We discovered later that the pillow he was using was stuffed with feathers. Nothing made John so allergic as feathers! His neighbors called the doctor, who was sleeping down the hall. She applied tourniquets to his arms and legs and got him to the ER down the hill at the AIM hospital just in time. He had minutes to spare, she told us the next morning. The two of us took a month to recover there at Kijabe. In some ways, John never did get over that trauma.

We went back to Scott College at Machakos for a few months, but John was too weak to manage his rigorous classroom-teaching schedule. We had a few months to go on our contract and we were not sure what to do. The Lord did. A crisis in Sudan turned out to provide a solution not just to our problem. We needed to leave Scott College early and two missionaries who had fled the violence in Sudan needed a place to live and teach. They moved into our house. The lady took over my courses on women's life and work, and the man took John's load.

With our prayers answered so perfectly, we were free to return to Lancaster for some much-needed rest and medical attention. What we realized rather clearly on the way home was that we needed to retire for good. There was a little hitch with that plan. We had no money, except Social Security from my meager wages, and no place to live. Our need seemed insurmountable, but we prayed for God to show us His plan. For too long, we had trusted Him and found Him faithful. Now, we were sure He would show us His faithfulness again.

Unknown to us, some of my dearest friends at Calvary Church were already organized to raise the $20,000 that we needed at the time to pay the founders fee for our acceptance into Calvary Fellowship Homes. Alice Rohrer was an administrator there, and she and Teen Scheirer teamed up to raise the necessary money. Teen and Bob Scheirer had been my friends from high-school days. Bob was the Minister of Music at Calvary then and Teen taught school in Lebanon, Pennsylvania. Their son, Dan, had married our youngest daughter, Lois, so it is fair to say we were close. Ed and Marion Hess also joined the fund-raising team, and soon the money was in hand.

It is not possible to express in words the gratitude we felt for what this group of dear Christian friends did for John and me. We were speechless and overwhelmed with joy the day we saw our new apartment. It wasn't quite ready when we first got back to Lancaster, but Mrs. Hottenstein opened up her home for those three months, and we were able to relax there and purchase the things we needed to set up a retirement home in Lancaster.

We truly thrived in that cottage in the midst of a rich fellowship of retired missionaries. And, the church loved us and honored us in so many ways. John taught Sunday School often and we had many opportunities to share the Lord's work in Kenya. I was thankful that I was in America for my father's one hundredth birthday and for his funeral shortly after that. John and I were relaxed and felt strong and healthy as the years passed at the Homes. I stopped nursing there when I was 70.

On Sunday of Labor Day weekend 1983, several years after we had settled into our retirement cottage, John went to teach Sunday School at the church. I prepared his favorite dinner of fried chicken. We went to church and ate a relaxed lunch. John then did what he always did after Sunday lunch – he took a nap. But, it wasn't his usual half-hour snooze. He didn't wake up till 3 o'clock. I was a little concerned, but I didn't bother him.

When he finally did get up, he came out and said how well he had slept and how good he felt. He wanted to take a walk and visit the neighbors, so I got my coat while he went back to the bedroom to put on his shoes. Just as I reached for the door handle, I heard a loud thump. Strange, I thought – what could that be? I stepped back to see John lying on the floor on his face. I dropped to his side to locate a pulse. There was none. He had already slipped away, and I knew it.

I couldn't let myself believe it, so I rushed to the neighbor, who was a nurse, and she came over to confirm it. Yes, he was dead. But, I called 911 anyway. The ambulance came and indeed, he was declared dead on arrival at the hospital. He had suffered a massive heart attack when he stood up from tying his shoes and was gone before he hit the floor.

It was Sunday afternoon and my mind just swirled with a million thoughts as I went into shock. I couldn't sleep or eat. I did not know what to

Alice seated at the nursing station at Calvary Homes where she nursed until she was 70.

do. Pastor Crichton, the senior pastor at Calvary, was out of town. We had to wait for him to return on Wednesday. My son Steve came up from Texas and started making plans for the funeral with the church staff. The church family was in shock and disbelief with me. Some of John's family from Canada came down and took over making sure I ate and slept and kept a routine. Dan and Cathy were unable to come to the funeral because Kenya was in the middle of air attempted *coups de tat* on the very day John had died.

Thursday of that week, Calvary Church held a funeral service for a soldier of the cross who had fallen in their midst. I hardly remember the service, but I know that a huge crowd gathered to honor John. There were so many who came that the chapel was packed. John was laid to rest in the Landis family burial ground in the Schaeffer Cemetery in Elizabethtown. He lies next to my father and mother.

The one lesson I took away from John's sudden and unexpected death was that I needed to have a prepaid plan for my own funeral and burial. I could hardly function, let alone plan a funeral, and I did not want my children and friends to have the added stress over mine. Calvary Homes now requires all of its members to have an advanced directive on file. I have made and paid for my final plans.

It took me weeks to get any sense of normalcy to my life after the funeral. I just wanted to sit there and rehearse our life together and that fatal Sunday lunch. John's niece, Martha, came from Canada and

Alice being comforted in front of John's casket after a moving funeral service at Calvary church.

stayed for a week after the funeral to care for me. Then, Steve's wife, Penny, came up for another week and I felt more on my feet. My own two daughters gave me the kindest and most tender care during this sad time for them and me. We mourned together and yet, in their grief, they comforted their mother in body and spirit.

The four children came up shortly after Dan and Cathy returned from Kenya, and we cleared out John's things and rearranged my furniture. I wanted to move to a smaller, single-room efficiency and let a younger couple take my cottage.

I wasn't one to sit around and pine. I began to pray and ask the Lord for guidance as to what I could do with my regained strength and good health. Retirement in some recliner was not an option for me!

CHAPTER 11
The Next-To-Last Chapter

This is not the final chapter of my life. There is one yet to follow, and I hope to live long enough to blow out the candles on my one hundreth birthday cake before somebody else has to write it. This is, however, the last one I shall dictate, and it chronicles the efforts at ministry that I have made since John's death. Once a missionary, always a missionary, I'm afraid!

After living in Africa at a much slower pace, and after learning of the grace and hospitality of the people I once thought of as dark and primitive, I came back to America and was shocked at the decline of family values and the general moral degradation in our culture—especially in the media. Africa may now hold more "Christians" than America!

I was quite free to lend a hand to improve cultural and spiritual conditions here, so I was asked to run for an opening on the local Republican committee, which espoused a conservative philosophy and worldview very similar to mine. Some may wonder why I "got political," but something had to be done and these people looked like they were doing something. They welcomed me to join them.

For about four years, I was active on the committee, watching the polls, collecting absentee ballots and getting the humdrum work done that goes on behind the scenes of large campaigns. It was a thrill to see free speech work. The power of democracy, up close, was awesome. Africa has nothing like it and sorely needs it!

In the course of meetings and listening to campaign speeches and observing the social problems in Lancaster County, I came to the conclusion that the biggest need I could help meet was the need for an expanded prison ministry – warm bodies visiting and sharing with prisoners in cold cells. Many, if not most, prisoners were African American, and so I felt at ease among them. My heart went out especially to the women behind bars.

In 1990, I was privileged to be part of a Bill Glass prison weekend ministry. While in a local prison, I had several extended conversations with women in lockup for all sorts of reasons. They seemed most concerned about their children and what they were going to do once they got out. God laid a burden on my heart for them.

I began to pray about what I could do. I also began to talk and research what was being done for released female prisoners. I had to jump through a lot of hoops, but I began to make regular visits to local prisons to talk with the women, and to get a clear idea of how they thought and what they "really" needed – not including cash, cars and clothes!

There were release retraining programs, to be sure, but they were underfunded and understaffed. It seemed to me that what these women needed and never had was a mother who would mentor them not just in daily life, but in their spiritual pilgrimage – and for a decent amount of time. Just getting over the prison culture would take a lot of time, then they had so much else to learn. Worst of all, they could not make a mistake or they would be right back in their prison uniforms.

What they needed was what I was determined to provide – a house with a Christian dorm mother and a suite for each released woman. There, they would learn to cook nutritious meals, keep house, and apply rules for raising children with love and kindness, not a belt. They would be discipled in the faith. And, of course, we would have to help them find employment and manage their budgets.

It was a tall order for a woman of my age, but I had recruited a wonderful group of people who would form my board, help me raise money, and find just the right house to buy and begin our nonprofit halfway house.

It took me two years to get it all ready, but on May 30, 1994, Restoration House opened its doors and my dream became a reality. It would be more appropriate to say that my prayer was answered. Only God could have moved the mountains to make this ministry happen.

There it was! A beautiful two – story, classic home on a quiet street. I didn't get the country estate and huge lawn and shade trees I had ordered. But, we were able to rent a house that had room for three ladies in release mode and one civilian house mother. We initially estimated that it would take them three months to get through our entire training program and discipleship. We invited the first inmates to study the Bible, but we did not push them. Not a single one refused to take part in daily study and prayer.

Our first skill-training course included typing, answering the phone and greeting people. They also learned to balance a checkbook. Without those skills, they had almost no chance of getting hired or keeping their houses in order. We arranged job interviews for them and tried to counsel them when they ran into trouble with fellow workers or bosses.

Our biggest challenge turned out to be getting them on their feet enough to take back custody of their children. A mom who has a prison record most assuredly has a record of domestic strife first. Many of these women had no real fathers or they had abusive parents. We could teach them and they could practice positive behaviors for our benefit, but we could not control what happened once they left.

By the end of 1994, Restoration House was a fully accredited nonprofit with a license to operate a halfway house for prison women. Calvary Church members individually contributed food, furniture and financial support for this ministry. We employed a wonderful young Christian woman, Karen White, who also acted as the project director. It was her privilege to mentor our prison ladies. All was on track for expansion and we began to look for a bigger home to accommodate more women.

It should have been no surprise that if things were going so well, we could expect some interference from the dark side. About two years into this project to shed the light of the Word into the hearts of hard women, the Lord of Darkness himself moved in to put out the light of our ministry. The property we were renting changed hands and the new owner did not want the house used for this work. Furthermore, the neighbors were stirred up by the new owner to protest what they thought was our housing "criminals." The standard cry against such risky services is: "Not in my back yard" (NIMBY). It rose to a fever pitch, and we had no choice but to close up shop.

I remain sad to this day that such a ministry does not continue in Lancaster County. I was able to follow up on one of the girls with whom we spent a few months and she remains a believer. She is off drugs and alcohol, and has not returned to prison. How many more could we have touched in a lasting way?

In some ways, however, I can be philosophical about the end of that work, because I was getting older and it was time to stop driving and tearing around like I was a young woman myself.

I would have had to stop my work with Restoration House anyway, because in a short time, I had a stroke. I had gone out to eat at a restaurant one evening. The food I ate was tainted, I'm sure. The next morning I awoke and began to vomit, and then wretched so hard I had a stroke.

I became paralyzed on my left side for a short time, lost some hearing in one ear and struggled to regain my balance for months after. My oldest daughter, Joanne, came down from the Boston area to take me to her home to recover fully. There, she and Lois cared for me in the most tender and effective manner. I attribute my full recovery to Joanne and Lois' six months of constant care and good food. We forget when we are young that we are parents of our children for a time, but then they will become our parents in due time. Both girls continue to be attentive and generous to me. What a pleasure my grandchildren have been in my later life. They honor me with their laughter, playfulness and gifts. I am young again in their presence.

In October, 2008, on the occasion of my 90th birthday, Lois arranged with Moody Bible Institute to confer my belated diploma on me. Over sixty years after I had left the school, the executive director of alumni, Dr. Walter White, came to Calvary Church and presented me with an honorary diploma. The notation that came with the award said:

Moody Bible Institute, founded by DL Moody in 1886
Awards this honorary diploma to Alice E. Schellenberg
In testimony to her time of studies in the Missionary Course
And in appreciation of her Christian character and
Her lifetime of service in practical Christian ministry,
Given at Chicago, Illinois, this 20th day of October, 2002.

How much longer I have to live, I do not know. I have lived a long and full life, and I suppose it is proper for me to reflect on the entire scope of it here in these last few paragraphs. I have stitched together many patches, or vignettes that make up the fabric of my life. What does it mean as a whole?

> ### 65 Years Later, a Former Moody Student Receives an Honorary Diploma
>
> Sixty-five years after she left Moody, Alice Schellenberg received an honorary diploma, the day before her 95th birthday. In the presence of her family, friends, and church congregation, the Moody Alumni Association presented Schellenberg an honorary diploma at the Calvary Friendship Retirement Home in Lancaster, PA, where she currently lives. She said with a gentle smile, "I am speechless; this is the last thing I thought would happen." Overwhelmed by memories and appreciation, Schellenberg's eyes welled with tears several times as she shared her story.
>
>
> Alice Schellenberg receives her honorary diploma from Walter White

Alice receives her diploma from Moody's Director of Alumni affairs 65 years after leaving Moody for the mission-field.

I cannot think of better words to express the wisdom I have derived from this life and so many experiences like those contained in this book than the very same verses that have guided me all these years from the Word of God. From my early days at Moody until this day in my private room at Calvary Fellowship Homes, the single most important reference in Scripture for me has been the verses from Exodus 23:20: "Behold I send an Angel before thee, to keep thee in the way, and to bring thee unto the place which I have prepared."

There were times when I could not see around the corner to know what the place that my God had prepared for me looked like, but I came to trust this verse so deeply that I knew it would be a good place when I got there—even when getting there was not so pleasant. I know without a worry that the final place He has prepared for me is a good and lovely place as well.

We live in turbulent times. Many hearts are troubled and strong men faint. My life was not always a bed of roses and there were times when I fainted, too. Can you believe with me the verse from Romans 8:28 that says: "All things work together for good to those who love God and are called according to His purpose?"

I pray that my testimony recorded here will strengthen your courage and faith to trust God regardless of what you may go through.

Alice Schellenberg
Lancaster, Pennsylvania
November 2011